Richard Graves, Edward Holdsworth

The Reveries of Solitude

Consisting of Essays in Prose

Richard Graves, Edward Holdsworth

The Reveries of Solitude
Consisting of Essays in Prose

ISBN/EAN: 9783744689397

Printed in Europe, USA, Canada, Australia, Japan

Cover: Foto ©Thomas Meinert / pixelio.de

THE

Reveries of Solitude.

BY THE EDITOR OF

COLUMELLA, EUGENIUS, &c.

THE

Reveries of Solitude:

CONSISTING OF

ESSAYS IN PROSE,

A new Translation of the MUSCIPULA,

AND

ORIGINAL PIECES IN VERSE.

BY THE

EDITOR OF COLUMELLA, EUGENIUS, &c.

BATH, PRINTED BY R. CRUTTWELL,

FOR

G. G. J. AND J. ROBINSON, PATER-NOSTER-ROW,
LONDON. MDCCXCIII.

L'homme qui vive dans la Solitude,
(Pensant plus et agissant moins)
Eprove a certain age, " le besoin
D'ecrire."———

St. Flour, par M. de F—.

DEDICATION.

TO

MAJOR-GENERAL

SIR WILLIAM MEDOWS,

KNIGHT OF THE BATH.

SIR,

THOUGH an unauthoriſed addreſs of this kind, eſpecially when prefixed to ſo trifling a work, may have rather an impertinent than a reſpectful appearance; yet I reflect with ſo much pleaſure on the many inſtances of friendſhip and civility from you and Lady Medows, during your reſidence for ſome years in our neighbourhood, that I cannot reſiſt the inclination which I feel to make this publick acknowledgement of my private obligations.

I am no ſtranger, Sir, to the delicacy of your feelings; and am convinced, that you would rather face an enemy than a fulſome panegyriſt. I will not therefore ſay in your abſence, what I ſhould not dare to ſay if you were preſent; nor enlarge either on your reſpectable publick character, or your many amiable private virtues; and only add my cordial wiſhes for your ſafe return to your native country and your numerous friends; amongſt whom, though ambitious of that diſtinction, I dare hardly preſume to claim a place. I will beg leave, however, to ſubſcribe myſelf, with ſincere regard,

Your obliged

and obedient

humble ſervant,

THE AUTHOR.

Nov. 5th, 1792.

CONTENTS.

ORIGINAL RHYMES.

JUVENILITIES, EPIGRAMS, &c.

PART I.

MORAL ESSAYS, &c.

INTRODUCTION.

AS curiofity feems to be the predominant paffion with the generality of readers, in this age; and as many people perufe a *new* book with as much fatisfaction as a *good* book; mere *novelty* of drefs may perhaps induce readers of that defcription to perufe the following *Reveries*; which, if they do not afford them much inftruction, may at leaft amufe them, as they have done the writer, in deafnefs and *folitude*.

As many people likewife will read a *fhort effay*, who would be difmayed at the fight of a long differtation or a political pamphlet; thefe Reveries have alfo *brevity* to recommend them. And though the fubjects have been treated by infinitely better hands, yet there are readers, who will comprehend a remark fet in a familiar light, who would be puzzled by a more abftrufe, though perhaps a more juft train of reafoning.

The author wiſhes indeed to have theſe eſſays conſidered in a moral, or in a mere *literary*, rather than in a *political* light. And if he has ventured too boldly (in the two *firſt* of them) to utter his opinion on what he reads in his "weekly Chronicle," he certainly will not enter into a controverſy with any man living. He profeſſes himſelf *contented* indeed with the preſent imperfect ſtate of human affairs; but wiſhes well to thoſe who, from *diſintereſted*, patriotic motives, are willing to improve them.

However, though he flatters himſelf that he is poſſeſſed of as much candour and philanthropy as moſt men, and would no more quarrel with any one for thinking differently from him in religion or politics, than he would for his preferring white wine to red; yet, as a good citizen, he cannot but condemn thoſe turbulent ſpirits who, without any regard to the peace of the community or the *preſent* proſperous ſtate of the kingdom, ſo induſtriouſly diſſeminate their Utopian ſyſtems of government, and endeavour to make their countrymen diſſatisfied with a conſtitution, which, if it does not riſe up to their ſtandard of *perfection*, has confeſſedly been long the envy and admiration, not only of France itſelf, but of every nation in Europe.*

If any one could produce a plan of government, to which five hundred different perſons would not make five hundred objections, I would vote for having it ſubſtituted in the place of our own. But who can liſten with patience to complaints of tyranny and deſpotiſm, in this country, where no Ariſtocrate, nor the King himſelf, can take a duck or a gooſe from the meaneſt ſubject; or commit him to the round-houſe, but in conformity to the laws of the land? Or who does not ſicken at this eternal cant about "civil and religious liberty," in an age when, with unparalleled indecency and outrage, people abuſe, with impunity, the legiſlative and executive powers, King, Lords and Commons? And where, not only religious ſects of every

* See De Lolme (a citizen of Geneva) his "Conſtitution of "England."

kind, but the professed *enemies* of *all* religion, publish unmolested the most virulent invectives against the religion of their country?

Yet one would imagine, from some outcries of persecution, that a second Duke of Alva was coming with his cut-throats, to establish the inquisition; or that the Sicilian Vespers, or the massacre of Saint Bartholomew, were going to be repeated in old England; where, however, " every man sits under his own vine and his " own fig-tree," or rather under the sign of " the bunch of grapes," or " the barley-mow;" and securely smokes his pipe and talks treason; and having harangued, till he is tired, on liberty and the " *Rights of Man*," goes home, and acts the tyrant in his family; perhaps without any regard to the " *Rights of Women*;" or to the *duties* of an husband, of a father, or of a master; to his wife, his children, or his domesticks.

25th March, 1792.

THE

THE REVERIES OF SOLITUDE.

ON HEREDITARY TITLES.

Εγκώμιον Νυθέτικον.

THE natural equality of mankind, whether real or imaginary, and the great inequality of their condition in ſociety, has been the ſubject of complaint and of ſurpriſe, to ſuperficial obſervers, in all ages of the world. That one man ſhould abound in wealth, and riot at eaſe in all the luxuries of life, whilſt others, with equal merit perhaps, are doomed to earn a ſcanty ſubſiſtence by conſtant labour, has been thought to impeach the goodneſs, and even the juſtice of Providence.

In like manner, the unequal ranks, and especially the *hereditary honours*, which have subsisted in most civilized nations, have been deemed liable to the same objections. That a set of men, by the merit of their ancestors, should be distinguished by pompous *titles* and peculiar *privileges*, and claim the homage of those who are their superiors perhaps in virtue, sense, or learning, has appeared equally unjust and absurd.

A little reflection, however, will soon clear up these difficulties; and shew the necessity in the one instance, and, *I trust*, the expediency at least in the other, that it should be so. Not to mention, in the former case, the various talents and capacities with which men are born; the industry, sobriety and frugality of some men compared with the idleness, intemperance, and extravagance of others, sufficiently account for the affluence of the former, and for the unavoidable indigence of the latter. And what a man acquires by his labour, or saves by his œconomy, (and perhaps by denying himself many enjoyments to which he was entitled) he has certainly a right to *bequeath* to his descendants.

For a similar reason, if a man, by his extraordinary exertions, by his courage or his wise conduct, and perhaps by sacrificing his *health*, his *ease*, and the *common* enjoyments of life, has eminently served his coun-

try,

try, and, as a reward for ſuch tranſcendent merit, has been honoured with an illuſtrious title; it would certainly be the higheſt injuſtice, as well as a diſcouragement to the like exertions in others, to deprive his *family* of thoſe honours, for *whoſe* ſake alone perhaps he accepted of ſo unſubſtantial a recompence.*

In the caſe of an hereditary fortune, indeed, we too often ſee the heir ſquander away, in vice and extravagance, the fruits of his father's induſtry and frugality: and if he prefers a life of poverty and ſhame to one of credit and affluence: it is his own affair; he is his own maſter; and who has a right to controul him?

The ſame is applicable, it ſhould ſeem, to hereditary titles. If the deſcendant, by his worthleſs conduct, is determined to diſgrace his noble anceſtors, he renders himſelf doubly wicked and contemptible; both by ſwerving from ſuch bright examples, and by his profligacy exhibiting ſo ſhameful a contraſt to their patrio-

* The ingenious Mrs. Woolſtonecroft [*Rights of Women, paſſim*] is equally an enemy to *hereditary wealth* and hereditary titles: but if a man by his honeſt induſtry acquires a fortune, to whom is he to leave it;—to his own children, or to ſome family who by idleneſs or extravagance are reduced to poverty? When ſhe aſcribes the corrupt ſtate of ſociety to the *unequal ranks* into which it is diſtinguiſhed, ſhe miſtakes the cauſe for the effect—as the vices of ſome and the virtues of others will always produce that inequality.

tick virtues. Yet there does not ſeem to exiſt any power competent, in an *equitable view*, to deprive *another generation* of thoſe honours of which they may be more worthy, and even be excited, by their very titles, to act nobly and retrieve the credit of their family.

"Yes: the National Aſſembly, in a neighbouring country, has not only done thus, but has aboliſhed all diſtinctions of this kind for ever." Nay, to ſecure their *liberty*, ſo little regard has been ſhewn to *property* of any kind, that they have deprived the very provinces of the names which they have ſo long enjoyed; and inſtead of Dauphiny or Languedoc, which convey to the imagination of a foreigner the romantick ideas of vine-clad hills and beautiful foreſts, we hear of nothing but arithmetical diviſions, diſtricts, ſections, and municipalities, which convey no idea at all.*

Every Engliſhman muſt rejoice, that twenty millions of his fellow-creatures are emancipated from a ſyſtem of deſpotiſm, which was become abſolutely intolerable; and muſt honour that Aſſembly which aboliſhed lettres de

* As for titles of reſpect, they ſeem to have adopted the ludicrous part of quakeriſm, without their piety or virtue. Mr. Preſident muſt laugh at being called *Citizen* Preſident; as my man John would, if I ſhould ſay, Citizen John, bring me a glaſs of wine!

de cachet, eſtabliſhed juries, and the like: and, if they are ſincere in their pacifick profeſſions, " of no longer making war for conqueſt," and as a proof of it would demoliſh their fortifications at Cherburgh, as they have done the Baſtile, all Europe would have reaſon to rejoice in their revolution. For every one muſt applaud the enraged multitude for laying open the dungeons of the Baſtile, even by violence, though it was accidentally attended with murder and boodſhed. Thus far ſurely every one muſt approve of the French Revolution.

But " there are two ways of repairing an houſe, (as my man Patrick obſerves) one is, to pull it down." As " the welfare of the people is the ſupreme law,"* they had a right perhaps, in this caſe, to redreſs their own grievances: and as the revenues of the Clergy were become enormous, they may be juſtified perhaps in appropriating part of thoſe revenues to the exigences of the ſtate; though they might, it ſhould ſeem, have made a diſtinction between the ſecular and the regular eccleſiaſticks. For though the monaſtick orders had a tendency to promote idleneſs rather than devotion, the pariſh-prieſts were ſurely an uſeful and reſpectable order of men. And, as *ſome* religion has been deemed by the wiſeſt legiſlators as eſſential to the good of ſociety, I do

* Salus populi eſt ſuprema lex.

I do not think these philosophers can substitute a better in the place of the Christian religion. Besides, as the property of *peaceable* individuals, in all commotions, ought in *policy* to be held sacred, it would certainly have been better to have imposed a temporary tax, to any amount, than to have made such a body of men hostile to so good a cause.

But the uniting the nobility and the clergy in the same interest, by depriving the noblesse of their titles as they had done the clergy of their estates, appears to me an unaccountable measure, equally impolitick and unjust; alienating the nobility also from the cause of liberty, without the least apparent benefit to the publick. And never was Shakspeare's remark more applicable, than to such an act of injustice:

"Who steals my purse—steals trash—
"'Twas mine; 'tis his; and has been slave to thousands;
"But he who filches from me '*my good name,*'
"Robs me of that, which '*naught enriches him,*'
"And makes *me* poor indeed."——OTHELLO, act 3d.

If the present noblesse made a bad use of their privileges, or if titles were prostituted by *sale* to the wealthy, to exempt them from their proportion of taxes; such a shameful traffick, among many other abuses, might have been reformed: but why should the order be abolished?

Even

Even the venerable towers of the Baſtile, though the ingenious Dr. Aikin thinks the demoliſhing them "was a proper ſacrifice to recovered freedom;"* yet after the power of the crown was ſo far diminiſhed, they ſurely might have remained, as a noble ſpecimen of ancient magnificence, and an harmleſs ornament to the city; and even as a terror to future monarchs, and a *memorial* that the *ſtrongeſt fortreſs* cannot reſiſt the force of an injured and enraged people.†

I am aware of the ridicule to which I may expoſe myſelf on this ſubject, in ſo enlightened an age, and that ſuch remarks muſt be treated with the utmoſt contempt by the preſent prevailing faction; who, with truly Gothick rage, ſeem determined to deſtroy every monument of their ancient grandeur and of the fine arts: but I am one of the multitude;‡ and have a ſuperſtitious veneration for all other remains of antiquity—as well as for antient titles.

Without conſidering our nobility, in a political light, as forming a neceſſary part in the ſcale of ſubordination; or in their legiſlative capacity, as a barrier againſt royal

---

* Life of Howard.

† The people, however, are now the tyrants; and the well-meaning King feels the horrors of the *Baſtile* for wiſhing to partake of the *liberty* which his ſubjects enjoy.

‡ Unus multorum. Hor.

royal influence and popular incroachments;‡ I look upon our nobility as a ſort of hiſtorical ornaments (like columns or triumphal arches) in the annals of our country. Without regard to party, every Engliſhman muſt recollect with pride thoſe periods of their hiſtory, when a Burleigh or a Clarendon, a Marlborough or an Ormond, a Hawke, a Howe, or a Rodney, preſided in their councils, or commanded their fleets and armies; as every Frenchman, notwithſtanding the preſent rage for levelling all diſtinctions, muſt (one would imagine) hear with pleaſure of their Condés and Montmorencys; their Sullys, Vendomes, and other great names, which illuminate their annals.

An aſſemblage of huts and thatched cottages, ſuch as Cæſar repreſents the towns of our Britiſh anceſtors, might ſerve the purpoſe of ſheltering them from the inclemencies of the weather: but who would prefer ſuch mean accommodations to the preſent metropolis, adorned with temples, cupolas, palaces, ſquares, and exchanges, and other emblems of wealth and proſperity?

This may be thought ſomewhat declamatory, but it is conſonant to my feelings; and appears to me to be a natural ſentiment. I have an old oak, which caſts rather an unfriendly and even noxious ſhade over my kitchen

‡ See Blackſtone's Comment. b. i. p. 157.

kitchen garden; yet I cannot be prevailed on to cut down ſo venerable an *ornament* to my old manſion, notwithſtanding the remonſtrances of the advocates for the modern taſte, who would reduce every thing to a wild, unintereſting *level.*

But, that I may not be thought too blindly attached to the Ariſtocracy, I muſt obſerve, that when a man of rank is weak enough to conſider *birth* as *every*-thing and virtue as *nothing*; and, inſtead of politeneſs and condeſcenſion, treats with unneceſſary haughtineſs and inſolence, a man of ſenſe and liberal education; much more when he takes advantage of his privilege to oppreſs or defraud his inferiors; though even in that caſe, a virtuous and prudent man perhaps would only ſmile at ſuch folly* with ſilent diſdain; yet one of leſs ſcrupulous principles would probably return that moſt intolerable of all injuries—contempt, with rudeneſs at leaſt, if not with ſome more ſignal mark of reſentment and

* A friend has ſupplied me with the following jeu d'eſprit; which, though founded on a pun, has ſome truth in it:

"When *arms* to the peerage were granted by kings,
"*Supporters* were deem'd indiſpenſable things:
"To enable their lordſhips to walk upright and ſteady;
"For a coronet's apt to make the head giddy,
"A *weak* head, I mean; for it can't be denied
"That *folly* alone is the *parent* of *pride*."

and revenge. The folly of individuals, however, in any rank of life, ought not to reflect on the whole body.

But our present race of nobles and even our pr-n—s (it has been said*) are a profligate set of *jockies* and gamblers, extravagant and licentious, and, (what would not be expected) *ignorant* and *illiterate*.†

That the age, or rather the nation in general, is extremely dissolute and profuse; and that the wealth, brought into the kingdom by a most extensive commerce, has produced its natural offspring, luxury and every species of vice and extravagance, not only amongst many of our nobility, but amongst all orders and ranks of people, from the prince to the peasant, is greatly to to be lamented.‡

But

* History of the Jockey-Club.

† I have not been much conversant with our nobility, yet I know personally some few very young men; who, if they would unite in the cause of virtue and form a club in opposition to the Jockey-Club; and instead of drinking and gambling, would countenance manly conversation and temperate festivity; I should hope, that such characters as this author—in his history; or such fools as Ch. Sm-th has drawn in her novel, if any such now exist, will be deemed absolutely unnatural in the next generation.

‡ Have these rigid reformers themselves entirely escaped the contagion? and are *their* lives perfectly immaculate?

But ſhall the vices and follies of *comparatively* a few thoughtleſs individuals, the ebullitions of youth and high ſpirits, eclipſe the luſtre of a majority of great and virtuous characters, which conſtitute that venerable, and; as it has always been eſteemed, that moſt uncorrupt tribunal, the Houſe of Lords? Such as, without regard to party, we may pronounce a Beaufort, a Portland, and a Richmond: a Camden and a Carliſle; a Thurlow, a Grenville, and a Loughborough; and many more, whom for brevity's ſake alone I omit. Shall even the private or the publick vices, which party-rage may impute to individuals, I ſay, juſtify any author, in repreſenting that aſſembly as a pandamonium; or be a ſufficient plea for the attempts of diſſatisfied demagogues, to overturn the conſtitution?

But "virtue" (it has been truly ſaid, and for theſe fifteen hundred years repeated) "virtue is the only true nobility,"* the only diſtinction which renders one man ſuperior to another—and a title, "a mere nickname," and a coronet, a childiſh bauble, a ring of gold lined with cat-ſkin: trifles beneath the attention of a wiſe man.

True: but the diſtinctions, or the privileges at leaſt, implied by thoſe baubles, and originally beſtowed as the

* Nobilitas ſola eſt atq; unica virtus. JUV.

the *rewards* of virtue, have been thought no trifles by men of as much ſenſe as Mr. Paine, and others who have repeated thoſe trite remarks: and have been adopted, in ſome ſhape or other, by the wiſeſt nations, as cheap rewards for diſtinguiſhed merit.

"Gold and ſilver are the droſs or ſediment of the earth," (as the philoſophick Antoninus obſerves*) but when ſtamped by authority, they acquire, by the common conſent of mankind, a real value; and procure the neceſſaries and conveniences of life, which none but a cynick or a madman would deſpiſe.

To conclude theſe reflexions. Though I can hardly flatter myſelf that any perſon of rank, much leſs of *princely* rank, will attend to an obſcure recluſe; yet, as I profeſs myſelf an enthuſiaſtick friend to ſubordination and to eſtabliſhed forms, I ſincerely hope, that our preſent young noblemen will reflect, that the dæmon of turbulence and faction is gone forth; and levelling principles are univerſally diſſeminated through the world: and it highly concerns them to be careful† of their

---

* Meditations, b. ix. §. 36.

† "The toe of the peaſant comes ſo near the heel of the courtier, that he galls his kibe."——HAMLET.

their conduct.* All eyes are fixed upon them, and they are in some measure accountable to the community for the privileges which they enjoy; and, as they are so much elevated above their fellow-citizens in rank, they should outshine them in the splendour of their virtues. They have it in their power, even by their example, to improve the manners of the age, and to make frugality and sobriety fashionable; and, by that means, to render their pre-eminence respectable, and also less painful and invidious than it often is to their inferiors. They should reflect, that, although the Sovereign can entitle them to be *called noble*, Virtue alone can *make* them so. Their titles may procure them a forced respect, but good-nature and condescension alone can make them loved and esteemed.

In short, when those young men can spare a few months from the nocturnal revels of the metropolis, from plundering each other like highwaymen, and with gladiatorial ferocity meditating each other's ruin, in gaming-houses or on the turf; let them, I say, spend some part of their time, and of their *fortune*, at their

country-

* Nothing, I believe, has given greater offence, than the immense sums, said to be squandered away by some young persons of the highest rank; but, by the firmness of the ministry, a more œconomical plan seems to have been adopted, and the publick will not be further burthened on that account.

country-ſeats, amongſt their tenants and vaſſals: let them reflect, how ſmall a portion of thoſe ſums, which they laviſh on unmeaning diſſipation, and in "ſhape-leſs idleneſs," as Shakſpeare calls it, would afford them the heartfelt luxury of relieving the neceſſities of the poor, induſtrious labourers, in the neighbouring villages:—They would then appear truly and intrinſically noble, and revive that ancient magnificence, and reſpectable hoſpitality, (without the intemperance) for which our Engliſh nobility have, at different periods of our hiſtory, been ſo eminently diſtinguiſhed.

THE SEQUEL;

OR,

FURTHER REFLECTIONS ON THE EQUALIZING SYSTEM.

THOUGH I acknowledge myſelf but ſlightly verſed in politicks, yet having alluded to the preſent faſhionable theory of government, I think it neceſſary to ſay a few words on that ſubject.

As

As I have always admired Rousseau's *project*,* of forming the several states of Europe into one grand confederacy, and securing the peace of each by the guarantee of the whole; so I was much pleased with the simplicity of Mr. P—ne's system, as sketched out in his "Rights of Man;" and if this planet of ours had been peopled with angels, or even with philosophers, who, like his Americans during the war, would have been "governed without any government at all," Mr. P—ne's theory would probably have been as good as any other: but, as he professes to have drawn his "*political principles* entirely from *his own* reflections," I should be inclined to question the utility of a system which had lain hid from the foundation of the world, and had eluded the researches, not only of the Solons, the Numas, and all the sages of antiquity; but even of our Harington, Sidney, and Locke; and has been reserved as a mystery revealed only to an uneducated English refugee. But the argument from his own experience and observation, during the American war, "how easily men may be governed without any government," is very fallacious; for they were really, a great part of the time, under a *military* government; and considering how firmly they were united, by a sense

* Whether Henry IV. had any such view or not, Rousseau might take the hint from the same project which some statesmen have imputed to him.

whether of real or fancied injuries, and with what *enthusiasm* they were animated in the pursuit of their favourite object of independence; we cannot be surprized that they had no leisure to quarrel among themselves, or to injure each other.

But (though Agrarian laws have always been accounted unjust) yet let us suppose the possessions of the frugal and industrious to be divided amongst the idle and extravagant; as boys, who have eaten their cake first, claim part with those who have been more saving and abstemious; and let us suppose, I say, this equalizing system to be realized in its *utmost extent*; let the patriarchal law of primogeniture be abolished; all distinction of ranks confounded; and, in short, a perfect equality prevail in *all the nations* of the world:—Let us suppose, as a familiar instance, in our own country, a gentleman possessed of an estate of one thousand pounds a year, to have ten children; and, instead of bequeathing the bulk of his estate to the eldest son, charged with a kind of paternal authority to inspect the education of the younger, (on the premature death of the parent) and also with a competent provision to establish them in some useful profession: let us suppose him, I say, to dismember the family estate, and to give to each child his proportion of an hundred pounds a year; what would probably be the consequence? Why; they would cultivate

vate their little farms, you will ſay; or employ their property in trade, manufactories, or commerce. But whom would they get to plough and ſow; reap, or threſh out their corn? For, upon a ſuppoſition of *univerſal* equality, every one would be employed about his own buſineſs, and in providing for his own neceſſities. And in manufactories, who would be maſter, and who would do the drudgery; ſweat at the forge or the anvil; or handle the file and the hammer?* And in trade, if all were ſellers, who would be the buyers or purchaſe their manufactures? For indeed, as there would be no diſtinction of rank, all the ſuperfluities and luxuries of life would be given up; ſo that the elegant, if not the uſeful mechanick arts muſt ſoon be loſt, and commerce itſelf be extinguiſhed.

Beſides, if every one were thus upon a level, no government, it ſhould ſeem, could poſſibly ſubſiſt. For who would obey half a dozen ſavages, dreſſed in ſheepſkins, (for taylors there would be none) ignorant, and in every reſpect no better than themſelves. In ſhort, if it were *poſſible* for this univerſal equality to ſubſiſt for any time in all the nations of the world; as every one muſt then be *entirely occupied* in providing for his mere ſub-

 ſiſtence,

* That is, upon a ſuppoſition that this equality univerſally prevailed.

ſiſtence, all the arts and ſciences would by degrees be loſt, and mankind relapſe into its primitive ignorance and barbarity. This, however, is the golden age, which an ingenious pupil of Mr. P—ne's ſo ardently wiſhes to ſee; "When there will be no diſtinctions of rich "and poor,—of maſter and ſervant; but every man "will cheerfully labour to provide for himſelf the ne-"ceſſaries of life; and, being content with *mere neceſ-"ſaries*, will employ his *leiſure* hours, (which, however, "would probably be but few) in ſublime *ſpeculations*, "and in the *ſearch* of truth and wiſdom."*

"There will be no ſuch thing as private property;" but "every thing would be the property of him that "wanted moſt," (even ſuppoſe it to be a poor diſtreſſed highwayman;) of courſe "there would be a commu-"nity of wives;" ſo that he who found himſelf moſt in want of a wife, might ſeize upon the firſt woman he met; ["*ut in grege taurus.*" HOR.]—like the bull in a herd of cows.

As

* See Novel of ANNA St. IVES.—I was a ſtranger to Mr. *H—lcr—t's* perſon when this was written. He is an ingenious and worthy man; but of a delicate frame, and better calculated for the *ſearch of truth*, than to "labour for the neceſſaries of life;" and is himſelf a proof, that nature never intended—all men for the ſame occupation. May Mr. Holcroft long continue to entertain the publick by his admired dramatick works, and leave the mattock and the ſpade to more athletick conſtitutions!

As for a due ſubmiſſion to government, Mr. P—ne ſuppoſes men would be taught "to deſpiſe all external "grandeur, and the pageantry of courts; and to pay "no regard but to the intrinſick merit of their elected "magiſtrates."

We are apt to judge of other people's improvement by our own progreſs in knowledge; and of their good diſpoſition, by the goodneſs of our own hearts; as I make no doubt is the caſe with Mr. Holcroft, and, I would hope, with Mr. P—ne. And becauſe at an advanced age we find ourſelves more enlightened, and can deſpiſe the vain pomp of the world, we fancy every one we meet does the ſame. But, alas! the precepts of philoſophy cannot always ſubdue our paſſions, nor does our practice neceſſarily correſpond with our knowledge. How eaſily is the multitude miſled by intereſted or wrong-headed demagogues, even contrary to their true intereſt, and often to their own deſtruction! The hiſtory of popular governments abounds with inſtances of this kind: and without recurring to the melancholy events of former times, every one may recollect many recent examples in this country, within his own memory; and it is to be feared, what is now going on in a neighbouring kingdom will furniſh ſtill more inſtances, of the unhappy effects of being *governed* by *ungovernable* mobs and ſelf-appointed aſſociations. The French at leaſt,

it

it is to be feared, though ſufficiently enlightened to become ſenſible of their late abject ſlavery, have not virtue enough to be truſted with their freedom; but, like the Romans, in the time of Marcus Brutus, will want another tyrant, with a ſtrong military force, to keep them in awe:* as a maniac is ſafer under a keeper in his dark *cell*, than when let looſe to the conduct of his own diſtorted imagination. But what ſtronger argument can we have againſt the happineſs of a democratick government, than from Mr. P—ne's favourite republick of Athens? which was perpetually rent by feuds and factions; and where every man that was eminent for his virtues, or diſtinguiſhed for his zeal in the ſervice of his country, inſtead of being rewarded with a title, was ſure to end his days in baniſhment or in a priſon; as Miltiades, Themiſtocles, Ariſtides, Phocion, and many others really did.† If it be ſaid, that by this jealous vigilance, they ſecured their *freedom*,—I anſwer, that

* The Romans, after the expulſion of their kings, are often ſaid, to have been a *free* people; but were they a *happy* people? What period of their hiſtory can we fix upon (when they were not engaged in foreign wars) that they were free from civil commotions? When their conqueſts were extended, and their wealth increaſed, their forums or great ſquares, and their field of Mars, were fields of blood.

† Ariſtides was confeſſedly baniſhed for having diſtinguiſhed himſelf amongſt his fellow-citizens by his ſtrict regard to *juſtice*.

that the moſt deſpotick monarchy cannot be worſe than ſuch a *nominal freedom*, which expoſes a man to the caprice of that many-headed monſter, a ferocious, tyrannical populace.*

In ſhort, notwithſtanding the late extraordinary diſcoveries in politicks, I cannot but conclude that ſome kind of *ſubordination* is eſſential to government; and that ſome little myſtery in the adminiſtration of it is more conducive to the good of the whole, than that familiar intercourſe between the governors and the governed, which this boaſted equality holds forth, and where the well-informed and the ignorant have an equal right to give their opinions, and to perplex and impede the operations of government. Mr. Paine's plauſible maxim, "That all men are born equal," ſeems now generally underſtood and exploded by people of ſenſe. All men are born with an equal *right* to liberty and property; yet none but a madman would ſay, that they are born with equal capacities and talents fit for places of truſt or publick employment. His pernicious doctrines, however, have diffuſed ſuch a ſpirit of

* Since this was ſent to the preſs, the French populace have perpetrated ſuch horrid maſſacres, under a pretence of ſecuring their liberty, that I hope, we ſhall hear no more of the miſchief aſcribed to fanaticiſm or religious fury.

" Tantum *libertas* potuit ſuadere malorum. LUCRET.

of disobedience to lawful authority, as is destructive of all government. However, though the people are so industriously taught, not only to "*speak evil* of dignities, but to *laugh* at them," I would by no means wish to see the *ensigns* of power abolished; nor advise our judges to lay aside their furs or solemn wigs; our nobility their parliamentary robes; or even the clergy their decent habiliments; which, when vested with legal authority, and supported "by inward greatness, unaffected wisdom, and sanctity of manners," must have a beneficial influence on society, and tend to keep in awe the most profligate offenders.

The Romans, in the purest ages of the republick, had their ensigns of office, their ivory chair, their robe of state, their *fasces*, and the like. And if any buffoon had dared to ridicule even that bundle of faggot-sticks carried before the Consuls, he would probably, in that *free* state, have been severely scourged with the rods, and perhaps have felt the keen edge of the axe, which was bound up in the midst of them.

POSTSCRIPT.

As the present situation of the Royal Family of France engages universal attention, I cannot forbear inserting the following extract from Dr. Adam Smith, on distinction of ranks:

"That

" That kings are the ſervants of the publick (ſays " he) is the doctrine of reaſon and philoſophy; but it " is not the doctrine of nature. Their conduct muſt " have excited the higheſt degree of fear, hatred, and " reſentment, before the bulk of the people can be " brought to oppoſe them, or deſire to ſee them pu- " niſhed or depoſed: even when they have been brought " this length, they are apt to relent, and relapſe into " their habitual ſtate of deference to thoſe whom they " have been accuſtomed to look upon as their natural " ſuperiors. Compaſſion ſoon takes place of reſent- " ment: they forget all paſt provocations, and return " to their old principles of loyalty and ſubmiſſion. " The death of Charles the firſt brought about the " reſtoration of the Royal Family."

Moral Sent. vol. I. p. 128.

See alſo a curious account from Plutarch, of the triumph of Paulus Emilius over the king of Macedon, page 134.

OFFICIOUS DEMAGOGUES.

TOWARDS the end of laſt autumn, I ſpent a month with an old acquaintance in the country: he is the clergyman of a large village, in a ſequeſtered valley, inhabited chiefly by ſubſtantial farmers, and the cottagers employed by them in the cultivation of their farms. As I am an early riſer, I was highly gratified to obſerve with what cheerfulneſs and alacrity they all went out in the morning to their reſpective employments: the plowman whiſtling after his team; the woodman with his bill-hook, followed by his faithful cur; the milk-maid ſinging beneath her cow; and the ſober farmer ſuperintending the whole: and on a Sunday attending the publick worſhip, as their anceſtors had done before them; and reſpectfully bowing to their rector as he paſſed by them, entirely ſatisfied with the *plain* doctrine with which he ſupplied them. And ſuch is the caſe, I am perſuaded, in many of the leſs-frequented parts of the kingdom, where luxury, and the examples of the wealthy and extravagant, have not yet extended their baneful influence.

Woe

Woe betide thoſe *officious* patriots, then, who, under a pretence of improving the condition of theſe contented, inoffenſive mortals, ſhall attempt to rob them of their preſent ſhare of felicity!

But, alas! as we rode over once or twice a week, to a large clothing town, at about five miles diſtance, we here found the publick-houſe, where we put up our horſes, filled with a mob of ragged wretches, belonging to the different branches of the trade, drinking pots of ale, and liſtening to a ſeditious newſpaper, (which, I found, was ſent down gratis every week) tending to perſuade them, "that the nation was on the brink of "ruin; that trade was languiſhing under the burthen "of our taxes; and, from the defects in our *conſtitution*, "and the bad management of publick affairs, there "were no hopes, without ſome *great change*, of better "times."

I aſked a clothier, with whom my friend was acquainted, why thoſe poor people appeared ſo wretched? and whether their trade was really on the decline?—It was never more flouriſhing, ſaid he: and thoſe fellows might live as happily as any people in the kingdom, but that every Monday morning they ſpend half their week's wages, which they receive on Saturday night, in an ale-houſe, regardleſs of the remonſtrances of their wives,

wives, and the cries of their children; and then complain of the taxes, and liſten to any one who would perſuade them that the fault is in the *conſtitution*, or in the publick adminiſtration, inſtead of their own idleneſs and extravagance.

There have been few governments ſo corrupt or oppreſſive, in which any great change or revolution has been attempted, without producing more evils than it was intended to remove. It is a well-known fact, in the Roman hiſtory, that more blood was ſpilt in *four months*, amidſt the commotions which ſucceeded the death of Nero, than had been ſhed in the *fourteen years* even of that moſt cruel and bloody reign. A fact worthy the attention of thoſe officious demagogues, who are daily diſquieting the minds of the people, and by indecent reflections on the moſt reſpectable characters, and inflammatory repreſentations of the (unavoidable) imperfections in all human inſtitutions, exciting them to riots and inſurrections!

Thus it was in the laſt century. Although from the reign of Henry the VIIth to that of Charles the Iſt, many encroachments had been made on the freedom of our conſtitution, yet theſe were now given up to the firm remonſtrances of ſome virtuous members of the long parliament. But, by the intrigues of ſome *officious*

or

or disappointed patriots, the people, who were in general rich and happy, were yet drawn in to cut each other's throats, in order to redress grievances, which, tho' they heard of, they neither saw, felt, nor understood. But

> "Hard words, jealousies, and fears,
> "Set folks together by the ears;" Hud.

and the contest was and long bloody, and ruinous to all parties.

In our present prosperous situation, some ingenious gentleman, who has nothing to *do*, and nothing to *lose*, sits down in his study, (his garret perhaps) and from visionary ideas of absolute perfection, forms a system of government, such as never really existed: which, without any regard to the peace or happiness of the *present* generation, but from a *tender* regard to *posterity* forsooth, some discontented statesmen or enthusiastick patriots would endeavour to obtrude upon their fellow-citizens by devastation and slaughter; and, under a shew of *liberty*, deprive thousands of their *property*; and, instead of reforming, destroy the constitution, dissolve the bonds which unite society, and introduce universal anarchy and licentiousness.

Such patriots, though their intentions may be good, are like anxious mothers, who, by officiously giving their

their children physick when they do not want it, debilitate their constitutions, and often bring them into a consumption. Such *state-quacks*, as they are properly called, with the most pompous and flattering professions, frequently *kill*, but seldom *cure*, their deluded patients.

If our constitution is a little out of order, and labours under any chronical complaint, let us not endeavour to precipitate a cure by *bleeding* and purging, or any violent methods; but let nature, assisted by gentle alteratives, do her own work. In James the IId's time, says the good Lord Lyttleton,* "A revolution became "*necessary*; and that necessity produced one." As no such necessity however now exists, let us not be trying experiments: nor quit a tolerable share of substantial felicity under our present constitution, for a phantom of perfection, which will for ever frustrate our expectations.

* Persian Letters.

ON OUR

TREATMENT OF SERVANTS.

THERE is no complaint more general than that of the ill behaviour and depravity of ſervants. Their negligence, idleneſs and extravagance, are reckoned by many people amongſt the greateſt vexations of life; inſomuch, that we frequently hear gentlemen declare, that they had rather wait on themſelves than be plagued with the ſtupidity or inſolence of their domeſticks.

Now, as human nature is much the ſame in all ranks of life, there muſt be ſome latent cauſe of this extenſive evil, either in the ſtate of ſervitude itſelf, or in the exerciſe of that authority which the ſuperior ſtation of the maſter gives him over the ſervant: I am inclined, from frequent obſervation, to place it, in *general*, to the account of the latter circumſtance.

It is become almoſt proverbial, that " a good maſter makes a good ſervant." There is no temper ſo obſtinate or untractable, as not to yield to the force of kindneſs and humanity; as, on the other hand, there is no one ſo meek or ſubmiſſive as not to revolt againſt continual ill-uſage and oppreſſion. Of this truth I ſee daily inſtances; and my two friends, PUSILLUS and POMPILIUS, will furniſh me with a recent example.

PUSILLUS had taken into his ſervice the ſon of an honeſt and induſtrious cottager, a ſturdy lad about fifteen—an age when iniquity begins to bud, and, if foſtered by idleneſs or not checked by wholſome diſcipline, ſoon gets beyond controul. His maſter, however, kept him conſtantly employed, and treated him with a proper mixture of ſtrictneſs and indulgence; and as the youth had good principles inſtilled into him by his parents, PETER ſoon became an excellent ſervant.

Encouraged by his neighbour's ſucceſs, POMPILIUS took another ſon of the ſame induſtrious family, who was a year younger than his brother, but equally ſtout, good-tempered, and well-diſpoſed. TOM was highly pleaſed with his preferment; and as his maſter lived in rather a more ſplendid ſtile, and gave a more ſhewy livery than Puſillus, and alſo thinking it beneath him to give too minute an attention to his ſervants, allowed him at firſt more idle hours; Tom exulted a little over his brother Peter, and excited in him ſome degree of envy. After a little time, however, things began to

wear

wear a different aſpect; and Tom felt himſelf not quite ſo happy as at firſt he expected. His maſter, by degrees, treated him with more haughtineſs and ſeverity; not only called him *names*, (as Tom indignantly complained) ſuch, as " whore's-bird and hang-gallows;" but threatened him with the horſe-whip for involuntary miſtakes; made him wait in the ſtreet for an hour with his horſes, called him away from his dinner, ſent him on errands at unſeaſonable hours in the night, or in rain or ſnow; and after all, would be-devil and be-d—mn him, without reaſon and without meaſure: whereas Puſillus (as any conſiderate maſter would do) often put himſelf to ſome little inconvenience, rather than expoſe his ſervant, without abſolute neceſſity, to hardſhips of that kind. But what are ſervants paid for? (cries Pompilius to Puſillus, who would ſometimes remonſtrate with him on that head.) " Oh; he is a ſad impudent, ſtupid dog, (adds he) and will never make a ſervant;" when Tom perhaps had imperfectly executed what his maſter had not condeſcended perfectly to explain.

In ſhort, the maſter and man ſeemed to live in a ſtate of perpetual hoſtility: the maſter lying in wait for an opportunity of venting his ſpleen on his ſervant; who in his turn, acting on no principle but that of fear, was more ſolicitous to avoid his maſter's reproaches, than to execute his commands, and gain his good-will. Pompilius indeed never *ſpoke** to Tom, but to abuſe him: and as ſervants have the ſame feelings, and, where they underſtand the premiſes, reaſon generally as juſtly as their maſters; how can we ſuppoſe, that ſuch treatment will not excite their reſentment? Accordingly Tom took every opportunity of retaliating on his maſter: and, as fellow-ſufferers naturally ſympathize with each other, whenever Tom met with ſuch a one, they would adjourn to a neighbouring ale-houſe, and vent their mutual complaints: this gave his maſter more juſt pretences to reproach him, and would ſoon alſo have brought on an habit of drinking; but, on ſuffering a violent outrage from his maſter, Tom gave him warning that he ſhould quit his place; who in his turn diſmiſſed him immediately, and refuſed to give him a character: luckily, however, a gentleman in the neighbourhood, who was on no terms with Pompilius, took Tom without a character, and, by proper treatment, has found him a valuable acquiſition.

Puſillus's man Peter likewiſe improves daily: his maſter calmly iſſues out his orders; inſtructs him in his duty;

* As an inſtance that ſervants *feel* the inſult of a contemptuous ſilence; Lord Anſon's brother had made the tour of the Eaſt, and when he came to Aleppo, his ſervant left him, and gave for a reaſon, that his maſter had not ſpoken three words to him in a tour of 3000 miles.

duty; and on every occaſion, convinces Peter that he has *his* intereſt at heart, as well as his own. Peter, on the other hand, from an ambition to pleaſe his maſter, does many things voluntarily, and without waiting for his maſter's commands: and, as he makes his maſter's buſineſs his whole ſtudy, Puſillus often finds his account in conſulting with his ſervant, who, as far as his capacity extends, ſometimes judges better than his maſter. In a word, Pompilius proceeds on the tyrant's maxim, "*Oderint dum metuant*;" let them hate me, ſo that they fear me. Puſillus's maxim is the reverſe, "*Colant me potius quam timeant*;" let them reverence me, rather than fear me. And they are requited accordingly.

I will not preſume to interfere with the ladies' *treatment of ſervants:* under *their* mild and gentle ſway, their female attendants are generally made their friends and confidants, and their footmen ſometimes experience more than a fraternal affection: and I am perſuaded that, in this age, no ſuch capricious tyrants as Congreve's *Lady Wiſhfort*, or other characters of that kind, now exiſt.

Neither will I ſay any thing of the ſervants in the more elevated ranks of life; as I am afraid, they ſuffer more from the neglect, or from the examples of their maſters, than from their ſeverity: they copy their vices, or are ſeduced by the luxury and extravagance which too generally prevails in ſuch families, to become luxurious and extravagant themſelves: and to ſupport their extravagance, when ſettled in the world, they become diſhoneſt, and abandoned.* And during their ſervice, as they are kept up a great part of the night, to attend their maſters at the gambling-houſes, or their ladies at their aſſemblies of different kinds, we cannot much blame them, if, to make up for their loſs of reſt, they ſeek for amuſements not more innocent than thoſe of their ſuperiors.

Until ſome reformation, therefore, takes place in the manners and modes of life amongſt the higher circles, in vain will the promoters of Sunday Schools, Schools of Induſtry, and other charitable inſtitutions, labour to reform the morals of the lower claſſes of people, which are infallibly corrupted, in the firſt faſhionable family that takes them into their ſervice.

I ſhall cloſe this eſſay with Seneca's excellent epiſtle on the ſubject, which not only breathes a truly Chriſtian ſpirit, but gives us too lively a ſketch of the enormous luxury

* The frequent burglaries or houſe-breakings in the metropolis, are generally conducted by the connivance of profligate ſervants.

luxury and pride of the Romans in that age: to which ſtate, however, we ourſelves ſeem to be rapidly advancing, and partly from a ſimilar cauſe—the importation of the wealth, the luxury and effeminacy of the Aſiatick nations; who will probably revenge the unprovoked injuries which they have received from the Europeans, by gradually corrupting the morals of their conquerors, and make them in their turns the prey of ſome more virtuous and more warlike invaders.*

SENECA EPISTLE XLVII.

TO LUCILIUS.

I WAS much pleaſed to hear, from ſome of your neighbours in the country, upon what kind and familiar terms you live with your ſlaves. It is no more, indeed, than I ſhould have expected from your good-ſenſe and enlightened underſtanding. But, are they really our ſlaves?—No: they are men; they are our companions;

* ——Sævior armis
Luxuria incubuit; victumq; ulciſcitur orbem.
Juv. vi. 292.

companions; our humble freiends. Are they our ſlaves? No: they are only our fellow-ſervants; if you reflect that we are all equally under the *dominion* of fortune. I cannot but ſmile, therefore, at thoſe who would think themſelves polluted, if they were obliged to eat with their fellow-ſervants.

But why ſo? Only becauſe a moſt inſolent cuſtom has made it neceſſary for the maſter, as he *ſits* at table, to be attended by a crowd of ſlaves *ſtanding* round him. He eats more than his ſtomach can well contain; and, while he is thus voraciouſly cramming his diſtended paunch,* his unhappy ſlaves dare not move their lips, or utter a word. The loweſt whiſper is puniſhed with the laſh. Nor are the moſt caſual or involuntary circumſtances exempted from ſtripes. To cough, to ſneeze, to hiccup, or to interrupt the ſilence of the company by any kind of noiſe, is a capital offence.

Thus the poor ſlaves remain the whole night faſting and mute. Hence it comes to paſs, that thoſe who are not permitted to ſpeak before their maſters, take their revenge by talking enough behind their backs: whereas thoſe

* The original has a remark, of importance to health, "that the belly being thus diſtended, loſes its tone (and, the periſtaltick motion being obſtructed) diſcharges its contents with more difficulty than they were crammed in."

thoſe ſlaves who have been indulged in the liberty, not only of talking in their maſter's preſence, but of converſing modeſtly with them, have often been found ready to ſacrifice their own lives, to avert any danger which threatened the lives of their maſters. They *talked* in their convivial entertainments; but were impregnably *ſilent* under the torture.

From the ſame abſurd arrogance, aroſe the proverbial expreſſion, " A man has as many enemies as he has ſlaves." Alas! they are not yet our enemies, but we make them ſo.

I forbear to mention many other cruel and inhuman practices on this ſubject: That we do not treat our ſlaves as if they were men; but abuſe them, as if they were beaſts of burthen: That when we ſit down to table, one is employed to wipe up the ſpittle; another to gather up the ſcraps, which drop from the drunken gueſts; one ſtands to carve the coſtly fowls; and with certain artful flouriſhes, carrying his ſkilful hand round the breaſt and the rump, ſhakes it at once, properly carved, into the diſh.

Wretched mortal, who lives for no other purpoſe than to cut up crammed turkies! Though he perhaps is more deſpicably wretched, who, to gratify his appetite, has

has this poor mortal taught ſo frivolous an art; which through neceſſity alone he ſubmits to learn.*

The ſum of my precepts on this ſubject is in ſhort this:—That you live in ſuch a manner with your inferiors as you would wiſh to have your ſuperiors live with you. Do not eſtimate men by their functions, but by their manners: a man gives himſelf the one; accident allots him the other. He may be a ſlave in his perſon, but perhaps his mind is free. Shall it be imputed to him as a crime, that he is a ſlave? Tell me, who is not ſo. One man is a ſlave to his appetites: another to his avarice: another to his ambition: and all of us are ſlaves to *fear*.† Here is a man of conſular dignity, who makes himſelf a ſlave to a wealthy old woman. Here is a man abounding in riches; he is enſlaved to a little artful handmaid. Behold our young men of the firſt quality, the ſlaves of actreſſes and ſinging-girls.

Now, what can be more ignominious, than this voluntary ſervitude? Let not theſe faſtidious fops, then, deter you from behaving with affability; or at leaſt, without any unneceſſary haughtineſs, even towards your ſlaves. Let them love and reverence, rather than fear you.

"What,

* Some inſtances of the abuſe of their ſlaves are here omitted.

† This ſeems to allude to the ſocial doctrine of the paſſions.

" What, then, would you have us give our ſlaves their liberty, and degrade their maſters from their ſuperior ſtation?"

He that talks thus muſt have forgotten that maſters ought to be content with what is ſufficient for the gods themſelves: who are only *reverenced* and *loved.* But *love* is incompatible with *fear.* Moſt wiſely therefore, in my opinion, do you act; who will not be feared by your ſlaves; who chaſtiſe them with words alone, and leave brutes to be governed by ſeverity and ſtripes.

N. B. Cicero, Pliny the conſul, and all the beſt and wiſeſt of the Romans, ſpeak of their ſlaves with the ſame tenderneſs and humanity. If ſlaves therefore are abſolutely neceſſary for cultivating our ſugar-canes; let us, for ſhame, treat them with as much humanity as thoſe did their ſlaves who were ſtrangers to the goſpel.

But, as Governor Trelawny ſaid (with a ſevere irony) forty years ſince, " What ſignify the ſufferings or death of a few *outlandiſh* men, if we can ſend better goods to market?"

A CON-

A

CONTRAST.

POMPILIUS and PUSILLUS (for thus their acquaintance diſtinguiſhed them) were neighbours in the country, and generally companions in town. Their ſituation in life, their family and fortune, were nearly ſimilar, and they were about the ſame age; but in their perſons, their turn of mind, their behaviour, and their general œconomy, they were very different. Pompilius was a jolly, round-faced man, of an intrepid air and unbaſhful countenance. Puſillus was a ſlender, thin-faced little man, of a timid and diffident appearance. The one gave you ſome idea of Falſtaff: the other of Simon Shadow, Falſtaff's recruit. In Pompilius all was lofty, bold, and magnificent: in Puſillus every thing was the reverſe. The former, in his dreſs, his equipage, and manner of life, appeared rather above his fortune: the latter, not from a ſordid, but from an unaſſuming temper, was almoſt in the other extreme. Pompilius rode a ſtately ſteed, and was always attended by a ſervant.

vant. Pufillus fcampered about on a little Welch poney, with a crupper to his faddle, ftudying convenience rather than fhow. "Send my fervant hither!" was Pompilius's language on all occafions. "Pray "did you fee *our man* Peter?" was Pufillus's lefs imperious manner of expreffing himfelf.

Pompilius called every one, even much his fuperiors, with great familiarity by their Chriftian names, Jack or Harry: Pufillus never fpoke to his fhoemaker, or his taylor, without the addition of Mr. Such-a-one! I muft beg you not to difappoint me.

At an ordinary or any publick meeting, Pompilius took his place as near the upper end of the room as he could do with any degree of modefty or propriety, while Pufillus was loft in the crowd at the bottom of the table, often unnoticed by any of his acquaintance. Pompilius, even among ftrangers, would rally Pufillus, and fhew his wit at the expence of his friend, who could frequently have made ample reprifals, but was checked by delicacy, or an extreme diffidence and want of fpirit.

In town, when walking the ftreets, Pompilius made not only the ladies, but porters with their burthens, give him the way; while Pufillus gave the wall to cinder-wenches and chimney-fweepers.

Come,

" Come, Pusillus, said his friend, you shall go with me to the bank, to receive my dividend:" it was to no purpose to plead, that he was engaged at the other end of the town: Pompilius seizes him by the button, and baffles all resistance.

At the coffee-house Pompilius bullies the waiters, who instantaneously attend, and he has the choice of the papers: Pusillus is forced to call twice or thrice before he can get his coffee, or any paper at all.

Pompilius dictates to the company, in literature or politicks, with oracular solemnity. " What is your opinion of the last new play?" said a gentleman to Pompilius. " Why, it has some merit, replied he: but the characters are not sufficiently discriminated." Pompilius had not read the play, but this was precisely the judgment which his friend Pusillus had given of it that very morning.

An article of intelligence, which the former said he had received from the *best authority*, the latter, without contradicting him, knew to be no more than a vague *report* of the day.

Pompilius frequently uttered, with great parade, the most obvious remarks as his own discovery. Pusillus often

often ſaid good things, but with ſo little emphaſis and with ſo negligent an air, that none but nice obſervers took notice of them. For, as Shenſtone ſays, " It is neceſſary to lay *ſome ſtreſs* yourſelf on what you intend ſhould be remarked by others;" yet Pompilius, as I have obſerved, often retailed his friend's remarks as his own.

" Well, ſir," ſaid Sir Stephen Stately, to Puſillus, " I have diſpoſed of my ſon at laſt, by the advice, and on an excellent plan of your neighbour Pompilius;" which, by the way, was the very ſame plan repeatedly propoſed to Sir Stephen by Puſillus; though not being earneſtly enforced, was entirely unattended to by him; who, pompous and empty himſelf, diſregarded every thing which did not come recommended in a manner conſonant to his own ſublime ideas.

In ſhort, Puſillus, though not inſenſible of his own ſuperiority, yet for want of a proper ſpirit, continually ſurrendered his own opinions to thoſe of his friend Pompilius; on which account the latter was eſteemed, by ſuperficial obſervers, a man of great ſenſe and profound erudition; while Puſillus was reckoned a poor ignorant and weak man, by thoſe who had not half his ſenſe or learning: nay, what was of more ſerious conſequence, he once had like to have ſuffered through a culpable lenity to a poacher, who had robbed his fiſh-

pond,

pond, of which he had the ſtrongeſt evidence; but being unwilling, on account of his family to proſecute him, a raſcally attorney adviſed the fellow to proſecute Puſillus for defamation; he then, however, exerted himſelf, and puniſhed the thief as he deſerved.

After all, Pompilius gained no more than a forced external reſpect from the judicious, or from ſtrangers; while Puſillus was really loved and eſteemed by the diſcerning few, who intimately knew him: for though, by too tamely reſigning his real conſequence, the latter (with courage enough on important occaſions) was often treated with inattention and neglect; yet the former, by aſſuming more than he had a right to, though poſſeſſed of good-nature and many good qualities, was frequently pronounced "a confounded impudent fellow!"

ON

PRIDE AND VANITY.

THEIR DISTINCTION.

PRIDE and VANITY are often confounded with each other, and in common ſpeech are uſed as ſynonymous to expreſs the ſame thing. But, though they are ſomewhat ſimilar, and may perhaps be ſometimes found in the ſame perſon, yet there is an obvious diſtinction between them.

Vanity is only too much pleaſed with itſelf; pride is always joined with a contempt of others. The *proud* man values himſelf on advantages, which, in ſome meaſure, he really poſſeſſes: the *vain* man flatters himſelf (and wiſhes to be flattered by other people) for perfections which exiſt ſolely in his own imagination. The former, conſcious perhaps of his rank, his fortune, or ſome ſhare of underſtanding, aſſumes ſtate, and looks down with contempt on thoſe whom he conſiders as his inferiors in thoſe particulars: the latter, reflecting

E with

with ſelf-applauſe on his imaginary perfections, is pleaſed with thoſe who confirm him in the deluſion, and receives with perfect good-humour and complacency the leaſt grain of incenſe which is offered him.

CELSUS is the proudeſt, and his brother LEPIDUS the vaineſt, man I know. Celſus, by a ſtately and important air, keeps you at a diſtance; Lepidus, by his complaiſant, pleaſant, and familiar manner, levels all diſtinction. Celſus is indifferent to the cenſure or praiſe of thoſe whom he deſpiſes; Lepidus ſolicits the admiration and applauſe of every one with whom he converſes. The one receives a compliment as his due; the other is thankful for it, as a favour or an alms.

Celſus, however, though he impoſes on thoſe who have leſs ſenſe than himſelf, is deſpiſed by thoſe who have more; Lepidus, though a child may penetrate into his foible, is rather pitied than deſpiſed. The former, by aſſuming too much, ſometimes forfeits that reſpect which is his conſtant aim. The latter, though his vanity cannot entitle him to reſpect, is generally beloved for his condeſcenſion.

In the ſofter ſex, indeed, vanity is often attended with more fatal effects than pride; as their vanity expoſes them to the ſnares of ſeducers, while a degree of

pride

pride often preſerves their virtue; yet each of theſe foibles, if not guarded by better principles, often expoſes them to ridicule and contempt.

In ſhort, the proud man is an odious being: the vain man rather an entertaining animal. The one inſults, the other diverts the company. The vain man ſhould be rallied for his folly, and laughed out of his abſurdity: the proud man ſhould be treated with leſs ceremony, and, if he had his deſert, ſhould be drubbed into better manners. The ſpectators, at leaſt, would exult to ſee a man, who aſſumes ſuch airs of ſuperiority over his equals, treated, by ſome blunt fellow, with the utmoſt freedom, and reduced to a level with thoſe whom he affects to deſpiſe.

ON

INTEMPERANCE.

"THE firſt phyſicians by debauch were made;
" *Exceſs* began, and ſloth ſuſtains the trade:"

Thus ſings Dryden, and the good ſenſe contained in theſe well-known lines may atone for the abſurdity of the following:

" The wiſe for *cure* on *Exerciſe* depend,
" God never made his work for man to *mend.*"

EXCESS is undoubtedly the cauſe of almoſt all our complaints; but *exerciſe*, when we are ill, would, in many caſes, *aggravate* inſtead of *curing* them; and though a phyſician could not *improve* the work of the Creator (for there the fallacy lies) he ſurely might *mend* or repair it when out of order. A country carpenter could not improve or finiſh a coach; but if a wheel, or even the axle-tree, were broke, he might certainly *mend* or repair it.

But,

But, though " I *honour* a phyſician with the honour *due* to his art," which is always uſeful in acute, and ſometimes in chronical caſes; yet I conſider *temperance* as the ſovereign preſervative of health, ſuperior to the moſt boaſted medicines, and which renders even *exerciſe* itſelf in ſome meaſure needleſs. As exceſs is the cauſe of a great part of our diſeaſes, ſo there are few which temperance will not prevent, or by degrees remove. Repletion overloads and oppreſſes nature: abſtinence relieves her from that oppreſſion, and reſtores their tone or elaſticity to the diſtended veſſels, and often ſtifles a fever in its birth.

We complain of unhealthy ſituations, unſettled weather, hereditary gouts, delicate conſtitutions, and the like: and there is ſometimes perhaps foundation for theſe complaints; but in general, we might more juſtly complain of, and (like Montaigne's friend) " curſe the Bologna ſauſages, dried hams and tongues," and other high-ſeaſoned food, in which we have too freely indulged: for temperance, I will venture to ſay, would ſecure us from the influence of thoſe accidental or local circumſtances; and even infectious diſtempers would generally loſe their force, where the blood was not previouſly diſpoſed to inflammation or putrefaction, as was the caſe with Socrates, during the plague of

 Athens,

Athens, and as Mr. Howard repeatedly for many years experienced.*

And as temperance would fecure mankind from a great part of thofe difeafes, which are faid to be *naturally* incident to mortality: how fatal are the effects of its contrary, intemperance! What numbers of worthy and ufeful members of fociety, in every profeffion, daily fall a facrifice to this deftructive evil! How often is genius, improved by the labour of years, blafted, in the meridian of life, by the baneful effects of luxury and intemperance.

Where are many of my friends and contemporaries in the Univerfity, whofe conftitutions feemed calculated for a century's duration? Where are my friends W——, Sh-—, B——, and others; the companions of my youthful ftudies and amufements? Alas! long fince vanifhed, the victims of *comparative* intemperance: for though they were apparently fober and regular, as well as ftudious young men; yet temperance muft be confidered in a *relative* fenfe, and proportioned to our conftitution, our way of life, more active or more fedentary, and to the exercife we have it in our power to ufe.

In

* See Dr. Aikin's Life of Howard.

In the ſtreets of Bath, the general reſort of the infirm, and rendezvous of the medical tribe, (for where the carcaſe is, there will the ravens aſſemble) when I ſee an hundred ſturdy chairmen groaning under the loads of bloated invalids; or, in the Pump-room, compare the miſerable, gouty, paralytick, and emaciated figures, with the youthful, blooming beauties, who have not yet injured by indulgence, or disfigured by coſmeticks, the maſter-piece of the creation, I involuntarily exclaim,

" Ye Gods! What havock does *intemperance* make " among your works!"

Young Cyrus, accuſtomed to the ſimple diet of the Perſians, was diſguſted at the Court of Ecbatane, to ſee his grandfather Aſtyages, under a neceſſity of wiping his fingers, after every morſel that he put to his mouth. What would the young prince have ſaid to the indelicacy of a modern epicure, who indiſcriminately devours fiſh and fleſh; high ſoup and ſauce; with oil, vinegar, and muſtard; ſoy and cayenne-pepper, and all the diabolical ingredients in French or Engliſh cookery? How can ſuch diſcordant materials produce that ſimple balſamick fluid, ſo neceſſary to recruit and preſerve the health and ſtrength of the human body?

It is from theſe refinements of luxury, that we ſee thoſe crowds of patients, whoſe complaints have baffled

the

the ſkill of their phyſicians reſorting to Bath, and other ſulphureous and mineral ſprings:*

> "Condemn'd to water for *exceſs* in wine."
>
> EUPHROS. vol. I.

Theſe reflections were ſuggeſted on ſurveying lately a group of theſe cripples in the Pump-room; when I was recognized by a little active old man, who, forty years ſince, had been a member of a club with me, at a tavern near the Temple, and was then ſuppoſed to be in a rapid decline; but, by a ſtrict regimen, had ſurvived all our jolly bottle-companions, who at that time ridiculed him as a miſerable milkſop. By his temperance and ſobriety, he had improved and preſerved to his ſeventieth year, a crazy carcaſs; while the others, by their luxury and intemperance, had ruined their robuſt conſtitutions; and had long ſince gone where the ſenſual appetites, it is to be feared, will have no objects for their gratification.

---

* "Ubicunque ſcatent aquarum calentium venæ, ibi nova "diverſoria luxuriæ excitantur." SEN. Epiſt. 89.

ON THE

GRADUAL APPROACH

OF

OLD AGE.

" EHEU FUGACES LABUNTUR ANNI." HOR.

THERE is nothing which we more reluctantly believe, or of which we are more mortified to be reminded, than that "we are growing old." We look daily in the glaſs perhaps, to adjuſt our perriwigs, or ſmooth our cravats; but ſeldom attend to the ſilent progreſs of our years, and the alterations which the hand of time is gradually making in our perſons. We advance from youth to manhood, and from manhood decline into the vale of years, to old age and decrepitude; but by ſuch imperceptible degrees, that it almoſt eſcapes our notice. Hence we behold ſeptuagenarian beaux and beauties of the laſt age inattentive to the depredations of time, and, with more than youthful levity, infeſting the reſorts of youth and beauty, admiring or courting admiration:

admiration: the gentleman gallanting, the lady coquetting; infenfible of the contemptuous fmiles, and farcaftick fneers, which their prefence calls forth from every countenance.

But, if we could fpare one hour of retirement amidft thefe fcenes of diffipation, it muft occur, one would hope, to the moft thoughtlefs beings, how much more refpectable a character they would fupport, by confining themfelves to the domeftick circles of their friends and neighbours, than by haunting thefe frivolous, though gay, affemblies; and, like troubled ghofts, "making night hideous" by their ominous countenances and portentous appearance.

Yet I would not wifh to lock up in a mufeum thefe venerable figures, like antique marbles or Egyptian mummies: no, let them, occafionally, frequent a coffee-houfe, or the daily tea-tables of their neighbours and acquaintance; or even go, once in a feafon, to a ball or affembly, to fee their grandchildren dance, and to vent their fpleen on the progrefs of luxury, and the abfurdity of modern fafhions, fo unlike the *glorious* times when *they* were young: but let their own parlours be their chief refidence; and the fociety of their friends, their confolation and amufement: let them inftruct their younger acquaintance with the remarks, and en-

tertain

tertain them with the anecdotes, with which a long intercourſe with the world muſt have furniſhed them; and theſe young people, in return, will reverence their age; and, inſtead of ridiculing, bear with and pity their infirmities; and, by a reciprocal communication of the recent occurrences of the preſent day, furniſh an innocent amuſement, and make their time glide inſenſibly away in indolence, chearfulneſs, and ſerenity.

" You've eat and drunk, and ſported now too long;
" Tis time to go, and quit the giddy throng;
" Leſt youth forget the reverence due to age,
" And ridicule, and thruſt you off the ſtage."

Hor. Ep. (anonym.)

Seneca, in his twelfth epiſtle, treats this ſubject with ſome humour:

" Wherever I turn my eyes, I behold evident proofs of my old age. I went lately to my Villa, a few miles from town;* and on looking over my ſteward's accounts, I complained of the expence of his repairs. My ſteward ſaid, it was not owing to any neglect of his; that he had done every thing in his power; '*but*, ſays he, *the houſe is got* OLD.' Now this villa was erected

* " Ad quartum lapidem."—The Villa where he died in the bath. Tacit. b. 15.

erected under my own inſpection. What then will become of me, if the very ſtones, my contemporaries, are going to decay?

"Being out of humour with him, however, I ſeized another occaſion of venting my ſpleen againſt my ſervant. Theſe plane-trees, ſaid I, have certainly been greatly neglected. The leaves are all falling off; the branches grown knotty and parched up; the very trunks rough and ſqualid with moſs. This could not have happened, if they had been dug round and watered. The poor man, piqued at my ſuſpicions, ſwore upon his ſoul,* that he had given all poſſible attention to them; but that the trees were grown *old*. Now, to tell you a ſecret, I myſelf planted thoſe very trees; I myſelf beheld the firſt leaves they produced.

"Turning towards the gate; 'who is that decrepid old fellow there?' ſaid I: though you have done right to place him at the door, for he ſeems juſt ready to be carried to his funeral.† But where did you get this carcaſe? What have we to do with conveying other people's ſlaves to their burial?

"Ah!

* Per genium meum.

† Alluding to their cuſtom of placing dead bodies in the veſtibule.

" Ah! ſir, ſays the porter, don't you know me? I am your *Felicio*: to whom you uſed to ſend toys for fairings at the Saturnalian* holidays; I am the ſon of your old ſteward Philoſitus, your *little favourite.*"

" Why, ſure the fellow's out of his ſenſes, ſaid I. He fancies himſelf a child: my little favourite, forſooth! Indeed, it may be ſo; for, I ſee, he is ſhedding his teeth.†

" Well; this at leaſt I owe to my country-houſe; that wherever I turn myſelf, when I go thither, I am preſented with memorials of my old age. Let me then embrace and bid it welcome. Old age, if we know how to make a proper uſe of it, abounds in pleaſures: or this at leaſt, ſupplies the place of pleaſures,—that *we do not want them.*

" What an agreeable ſtate of life is this! To have ſubdued our paſſions; and got entirely rid of our importunate luſts and deſires!"——

---

* Like our Chriſtmas.

† From old age, as children do in their infancy.

ON

SINGULARITY OF MANNERS.

THERE are few people of ſuch mortified preten- ſions, as patiently to acquieſce under the total neglect of mankind: nay, ſo ambitious are moſt men of diſtinction, that they chuſe to be taken notice of, even for their abſurdities, rather than to be entirely overlooked, and loſt in obſcurity; and, if they deſpair of exciting the attention of the world, by any brilliant or uſeful accompliſhment, they will endeavour to gain it by ſome ridiculous peculiarity in their dreſs, their equipage, or accoutrements.

Many perſons may remember a little foreigner, (Des Caſeaux, I think, was his name) who appeared daily in the Mall, dreſſed in black, with an hat of an enormous diameter, and a long roll of paper in his hand. His picturesque appearance tempted ſome artiſts, to make an etching of him, which was exhibited in every ſhop. I mention this gentleman, becauſe his profeſſed inten- tion was, he ſaid, "to attract the notice of the king, as he had done that of his ſubjects."

But

But we ſee daily inſtances of the ſame kind. One man ſports a paradoxical walking-ſtick; another riſes to fame by the ſhortneſs of his coat, or the length of his trowſers, or the multiplicity of capes on his ſhoulders, and the like efforts of genius and invention. I remember a young divine, ſome years ſince, not otherwiſe eminent either for learning or ingenuity, who wore his own ſhort hair, when every one elſe wore long wigs, "in imitation, as he ſaid, of Gregory Nazianzen."

It would be cruel, to deprive theſe gentlemen of their ſlender gratification in theſe harmleſs particulars; but when we aſſume any thing peculiar in our appearance, in order to diſguiſe our real character; when we affect an uncommon ſanctity and ſolemnity of countenance to impoſe upon the world; we then become more than ridiculous, and are highly immoral.

A Tartuffe indeed, or a pretender to extraordinary devotion, is not a prevailing character in this age: too many are in the contrary extreme; and, like Colonel Chartres, are guilty of every human vice—except hypocriſy. Even our Young Divines, though doubtleſs much given to faſting and prayer in private, yet "appear not to men to faſt;" but anoint their hair, and exhibit their roſy faces; and, by their dreſs, are not to be diſtinguiſhed from prophane ſportſmen or country

'ſquires.

'ſquires. I do not exempt the orators of the tabernacle from this deſcription; who, inſtead of the primitive locks of John Weſley, ſeem now to make female converts by their well-dreſſed hair, and dapper appearance.

Yet, in every profeſſion, there are ſtill pretenders; who, by grimace or affected ſolemnity, endeavour to gain the confidence of the vulgar; and to exalt themſelves above their equals in ſkill, and aſſume more importance than is their due.

However, if we muſt diſtinguiſh ourſelves from the reſt of mankind, let it be by our intrinſick virtue, our temperance and ſobriety, and a conſcientious regard to every relative duty; but, as we ought "to think with the wiſe, and talk with the vulgar," let us alſo act differently from a great part of the world in matters of importance, but conform to them in trifles. This is what Seneca ſo forcibly inculcates in his fifth Epiſtle to his friend Lucilius.

"I both approve of your conduct, and ſincerely rejoice that you reſolutely exert yourſelf; and, laying aſide every other purſuit, make it your whole ſtudy to improve yourſelf in wiſdom and virtue. And I not only exhort, but earneſtly intreat you to perſevere in this courſe."

Give

"Give me leave, however, to caution you not to imitate thoſe pretended philoſophers, who are more ſolicitous to attract the notice of the world, than to make a progreſs in wiſdom; nor to affect any thing ſingular in your dreſs, or in your manner of life. Avoid that prepoſterous ambition of gaining applauſe, by your uncouth appearance, your hair uncombed, and your beard neglected; nor be always declaiming againſt the uſe of plate, of ſoft beds, or any thing of that kind. The very name of a philoſopher is ſufficiently invidious, though managed with the greateſt modeſty and diſcretion.

"Suppoſe we have entered upon our Stoical plan, and begun to ſequeſter ourſelves from the converſation and cuſtoms of the vulgar; let every thing *within* be diſſimilar; but let our *outward* appearance be conformable to the reſt of the world. Let not our apparel be ſplendid or ſhewy, nor yet mean or ſordid. Let not our plate be emboſſed with gold; but let us not imagine, that the mere want of ſuch expenſive plate is a ſufficient proof of our frugality. Let us endeavour to live a better life, not merely a life contrary to that of the vulgar; otherwiſe, inſtead of conciliating the favour of thoſe whom we wiſh to reform, we ſhall excite their averſion, and drive them from our company; we ſhall alſo deter them from imitating us in any thing, when they are afraid that they are to imitate us in every thing.

" The firſt advantages which philoſophy promiſes are, a juſt ſenſe of the common rights of mankind, humanity, and a ſociable diſpoſition; from which advantages, ſingularity and diſſimilar manners will entirely ſeclude us. Let us beware, leſt thoſe peculiarities by which we hope to excite the admiration, ſhould expoſe us to the ridicule and averſion, of mankind.

" Our object is to live according to nature; but to torture our bodies, to abhor cleanlineſs in our perſons, when attended with no trouble, or to affect a cynical filthineſs in our food; this ſure is living contrary to nature. As it is a mark of luxury to hunt after delicacies, to reject the common unexpenſive comforts of life is a degree of madneſs. Our Stoic philoſophy requires us to be frugal, not to mortify ourſelves; but there is ſuch a thing as an elegant frugality. This moderation is what I would recommend."——

AURORA;

OR,

THE APPARITION.

HAVING lately had a very ſober party, to cards and ſupper, at my country-houſe, I got early to bed, before one o'clock: I ſlept ſoundly for ſome hours; but when I awoke, to my aſtoniſhment, I beheld a female figure, modeſtly clad in a light robe, with a mild, ſerene countenance; who, moving from towards the window, came and ſtood at the feet of my bed. I was going to ſpeak, and expreſs my ſurpriſe, when ſhe prevented me, and thus began:—

"Do not be alarmed, ſir: though I am now a ſtranger to you, as you have not ſeen me ſince you were a ſchool-boy; yet I was well known to your good father and mother, with whom I was upon the moſt intimate footing. I breakfaſted with them every day in the week, and ſometimes dined with them; and was a peculiar favourite with your excellent mother. I now come daily into your village, and am well known to the farmers and poor people, to whom I am a true friend; and they always rejoice to ſee me, as I put them in a way to get their livelihood, and by a wholeſome elixir, with which I ſupply them gratis, and by my conſolatory and cheerful converſation, keep them in health and ſpirits. Nay, the very birds of the air ſeem to know me, and expreſs their joy at my approach." —Aſtoniſhment kept me ſilent, and ſhe proceeded in her harangue:

"I ſhould have introduced myſelf to you, (however unwelcome) out of regard to your father and mother; but am now excluded, I find, by the expreſs orders of your near friend, this pretended widow, in her ſable weeds forſooth, (Mrs. Hecatiſſa Midnight, I think they call her) to whom you are of late ſo unaccountably attached; and who, it ſeems, has a particular diſlike to me, as ſhe ſlips away whenever I happen to appear, being conſcious that I outſhine and eclipſe her; and knows alſo that I was a friend to your family, and muſt be concerned to ſee her encourage you in revelling, gaming, and every thing that is bad. And indeed, ſir, if you do not diſengage yourſelf from her inchantments, ſhe will be the ruin of your health, your fortune, and your reputation. All decent people are aſtoniſhed at your infatuation, (for I will ſpeak my mind, now I

have

have got admittance) ſince, in ſpite of her ſilver creſcent, which ſhe wears, I ſuppoſe, as an emblem of her chaſtity, it is well known ſhe has been kept by half the members of the Houſe of Commons and of the gambling clubs, nay, has walked the ſtreets and been proſtituted to hackney-coachmen, pickpockets, and ſtreet-robbers. And here you have brought her into the country, to ſeduce your ſober neighbours, who formerly paid me great attention: but now there is not a gentleman in the pariſh, except the vicar, who ſhews me the leaſt regard, and I only ſee him once or twice a week, as he rides out with the 'ſquire's huntſman; for as to the ſquire himſelf, whom I uſed frequently to viſit, and who was always glad to ſee me, he now follows your example, and curſes me if ever I am ſeen at his door."

I was here again beginning to make apologies; and to pacify her, made her a compliment on her beauty; but ſhe proceeded:

"I am not come to court you, ſir; yet, as I can never get ſight of you, and have nobody to ſpeak in my favour, indignation forces me to violate the rules of decorum, and to ſay, that I think myſelf much ſuperior in beauty, ſprightlineſs, and every virtuous quality, to this harridan, whom you are ſo fond of; and have had more compliments paid me (even by the beſt poets of the age) without any other ornaments than a few wild flowers, than ſhe ever had in her jewels and ſpangles, which glitter about her autumnal countenance, and which (by the way) ſhe has only borrowed (if not pilfered) from an illuſtrious friend of mine;* which, however, ſhe never appears in but clandeſtinely, being aſhamed to wear them in his preſence or in mine.

"In ſhort, ſir, if I could once detach you from this Ethiopian queen, (as Dr. Young calls her by way of ſneer) I have the vanity to think that my charms, ſuch as they are, would make a proper impreſſion on your heart, and you would be unwilling to paſs a ſingle day without ſeeing me; and I will venture to ſay, you would receive more pleaſure, as well as improvement, from the company to which I could introduce you, than from your preſent connexion. I am a particular acquaintance and friend of thoſe celebrated and accompliſhed young ladies whom you uſed to talk of when you came from ſchool, called, as an honourable diſtinction, "The Nine Siſters;"† who, though no great fortunes, are as much courted and careſſed as any young women in the kingdom, of their humble rank and retired way of life.

"I muſt

* The ſun. † Aurora Muſis Amica.

"I muſt confeſs, indeed, that I am much leſs in vogue amongſt people in high life than I was formerly; and am ſeldom ſeen at the court end of the town, except by the Marchioneſs of B—, the Counteſs of C—, Mrs. M---, and a few more ladies of ſuperior ſenſe, and of a literary turn. Nay, I am ſorry to ſay that of late I meet with but little reſpect even in the city, except by ſome of the loweſt and moſt induſtrious of the inhabitants; ſo that I now ſpend moſt of my time amongſt the honeſt laborious peaſants in the country; who, I hope, for their own ſake as well as that of the community, will continue to regard me."

I liſtened with attention to her diſcourſe; and, notwithſtanding the few ſallies of reſentment, which only added ſpirit to her features, I was charmed with the character of native ſweetneſs which appeared in her countenance; and having now recollected ſomething of her perſon, I ſaid, with ſome confuſion, "that I was ſorry I had ſo long been deprived of her viſits, and ſhould be happy to renew my acquaintance; and added, that I now remembered having often ſeen her in my youth, and that my mother uſed to call her 'her dear Aurora;' but having unhappily got acquainted with the widow Hecatiſſa in town, I owned ſhe had engroſſed too much of my time and attention; that for the future, however, I hoped to ſee *her* often, and would take effectual

care

care to have her admitted, whenever ſhe would condeſcend to honour me with her viſits."

I was going on, when a glow of ſplendour, like the riſing of the ſun, ſhone around her, and flaſhed in my face; and ſhe vaniſhed from my ſight.

I drew my curtains more cloſely round me; turned from the window; went to ſleep again—till noon——and have not ſeen the fair Aurora ſince.

THE

GRAND PROCESSION!

CEDENT ARMA TOGÆ!

RETURNING lately from a tour to the Lakes in Cumberland, I ſlept at a great manufacturing town in the North; and the next morning, having viewed every thing which was thought curious in the place, I ordered my horſes to proceed on my journey; when my landlord aſked me, if I would not ſtay to ſee the proceſſion? What proceſſion, ſaid I? "Why, ſir, there has lately been eſtabliſhed here a ſociety, called *the true and reſpectable Taylors*; and to-day they have their firſt grand feaſt, and walk in proceſſion to hear a ſermon at the great church." 'What is the intention of this ſociety?' ſaid I to my hoſt? "Why, ſir, partly to raiſe a fund for the ſupport of their decayed brethren of the thimble; and partly to reſcue their profeſſion from the contempt and ridicule, which is ſo often,

often, and ſo unjuſtly, levelled at ſo uſeful a branch of the community.

As I ſuppoſed this to be an humble imitation of the Society of Free-Maſons, of which I have the honour to be an unworthy member, I thought there might be ſomething humorous in ſuch a cavalcade, and accordingly ſtayed to ſee it.

At the head of the proceſſion there walked a very young divine in his canonicals; whom, I found, they had choſen in preference to the rector, becauſe his name was *Taylor*. On his left hand walked the preſident, a portly figure! dreſſed more like a general officer than a maſter-taylor; having an immenſe hat on, cocked with an air of terror and defiance; his coat, with old-faſhioned ſtiffened ſkirts and large ſleeves, lined with crimſon ſilk, and adorned with gold buttons. After them walked the whole fraternity; but intermixed, as I was told, with ſome few woollen-drapers, as between them and the taylors there is generally ſuppoſed to be a ſympathetick connexion, or fellow-feeling. In the midſt of the cavalcade walked the ſtandard-bearer, with the flag painted with the arms of the merchant-taylors; namely, a tent between two mantles, lined with ermine; a lion in chief, to ſhew that even a taylor can be valiant on occaſion; but a lamb for their creſt, to denote the

general

general meekneſs and pacifick character of their profeſſion. The camels for their ſupporters, probably allude to the materials formerly made uſe of for buttons, called mohair, which is chiefly the hair of the camel.

When we came to the church, the young curate had ſelected pſalms and leſſons proper for the occaſion, and had taken his text from St. Paul's epiſtle to the Romans: "A *remnant* ſhall be ſaved." As this was the firſt ſermon preached before the Company, it was chiefly hiſtorical; but I was ſorry to hear the preacher, before a ſociety founded on brotherly love and charity, begin with ſarcaſtical reflections on our much more reſpectable ſociety of "free and accepted Maſons." He ſaid, there was a certain *upſtart*, pragmatical ſet of people, called Free-Maſons, who pretended to claim the precedence, in point of antiquity, to the reſpectable body of Taylors; but if any of them could read, (ſaid the pedantick prig) let them look into the very beginning of their bible, and they will find that Adam made uſe of a *needle* for ſewing many ages before we hear any thing of trowels or building. And as for their Temple of Solomon, which they ſo profanely introduce on all occaſions; have they never heard how many years the Jews worſhipped in tents or tabernacles, before the Temple of Solomon had any exiſtence?—He proceeded

to

to lug in St. Paul, as an ornament to their ſociety, becauſe he was a tent-maker; though he might as well have introduced Saint Criſpin as a taylor, becauſe he was ſaid to have been a ſhoe-maker.

In ſhort; I was ſo much diſguſted with the young man's pertneſs, that I was ſlipping towards the door to make my eſcape, when a ſort of tipſtaff came up, and whiſpered to me, that the preſident, ſeeing I was a ſtranger, deſired I would honour them with my company at dinner. I was pleaſed with the compliment, ſat out the ſermon, and accordingly attended them at the entertainment, which was provided for them at an hotel.

The firſt courſe was ſumptuous, though rather ſubſtantial than elegant: there was fiſh and fowl of many ſorts; a fine Yorkſhire ham, and a rump of beef; and between every two diſhes, cabbages or cucumbers, dreſſed in different manners, boiled, ſtewed, pickled or preſerved; and, in the middle of the table, an immenſe red cabbage of a beautiful appearance, near to which the flag and other enſigns were placed.

The ſecond courſe, amongſt other things, conſiſted of a dozen of ſmall-birds at the top, dreſſed with their feathers on the head and wings, which ſhewed them to

be

be goldfinches, called in that country "*proud taylors*;" at the bottom, and on each ſide, were a green-gooſe and green-peaſe, which *pun* I was not ſorry to ſee repeated, as it is a diſh I am particularly fond of.

As I was ſeated near the chaplain, I took an opportunity after dinner of expoſtulating with him, in a jocular manner, on the ſeverity with which he had treated the Free-Maſons.—"Why, (ſaid the doctor) I have no objection to any ſocial meetings, which are conducted with ſobriety and decency, eſpecially ſuch as have ſo good an object in view as the preſent has; but I am provoked to have a ſerious affair and a myſtery made of what every one knows to be a mere farce, as Free-Maſonry is." [I found he himſelf knew nothing of the matter.] I then aſked him, if he had ſeen a very ingenious treatiſe, lately publiſhed, on free-maſonry! "Yes, replied he; and the author had better have called it a treatiſe on rope-dancing; which, as Dr. Johnſon humorouſly proved, comprehends all the cardinal virtues, (Prudence, juſtice, temperance, and fortitude:) for the treatiſe you mention is only an ingenious diſcourſe on morality and religion. And if virtue muſt be ſaid to be founded on *Maſonry*, becauſe, in a figurative ſenſe, it depends on rule and proportion; it may as well be ſaid to be founded on a taylor's meaſure, and a pair of breeches may be an emblem of modeſty,

and

and a ſirtout of charity, as it often " covers a multitude of ſins."

To get a truce to the doctor's ridicule, I aſked the Preſident, whether their ſociety had any *ſecret*, which they communicated to their initiated members, as the Free-Maſons had: " Yes, ſir, anſwered the Doctor, (who I found was the champion of the company) the taylors have many and more important ſecrets than the pretended Roſicrucian *ſecrets* of the Free-Maſons; their cœleſtial cube; their immortal carbuncle or pyramid of purple ſalt, more radiant than the ſun in its meridian glory; which are no more to the purpoſe, than the red cabbage which you ſaw in the middle of the table. But theſe " *reſpectable taylors*" communicate, to the initiated, the true and important ſecrets of the trade founded on mathematical principles, for the uſes of common life; how to cut out a ſquare piece of cloth, with the moſt advantage to themſelves as well as to their cuſtomers, into elliptical circles, parallellograms, parallellopipedons, and all the variety of dimenſions neceſſary to make a coat or a pair of breeches."

I ſuffered the orator to harangue without interruption, when a young member, who ſat near the preſident, waxing mellow, began ſpouting Hamlet:

" But

" ———— But that I am forbid
" To tell the ſecrets of my priſon-houſe,
" I could a tale unfold, whoſe lighteſt word
" Would harrow up thy ſoul."

The Preſident, a little ſore, called him "to order!" But the chaplain, now alſo a little elevated, ſaid, "Why, Mr. Preſident, I believe there are ſome ſecrets of your priſon-houſe, called *hell*, (where, I am told, you now and then ſlip a *remnant* of cloth) which ought not to be diſcloſed. I had my pulpit hung with black cloth, with which my taylor (not any one of this honeſt fraternity) made me indeed a coat and waiſtcoat, but ſo ſcanty, that I could not wear them; and brought me home a rag or two, not enough to make a pincuſhion. But half a year after I ſaw my gentleman in a handſome black waiſtcoat and breeches, which a diſcarded journeyman aſſured me was a *remnant* of my eleemoſinary pulpit-cloth.

A droll fellow now began to ſing, in no very melodious voice, the old ſong,

" A tinker and a taylor,
" A ſoldier and a ſailor,
" Were once at deadly ſtrife, ſir,
" To make a maid a wife, ſir,
" Whoſe name was buxom Joan, &c."

And

And as moſt of the fraternity began to be very obſtreperous, and the waiter came round to collect the ordinary, I paid my half-crown, and was taking leave of Mr. Preſident, when, towards the bottom of the table, was heard a great uproar. My landlord, it ſeems, without acquainting the Preſident, had introduced a little weeſel-faced fellow; who, though he had eaten as much as nine taylors, refuſed to pay more than one ſhilling for his ordinary and extraordinaries. He ſaid, he had dined at moſt of the Revolution Clubs in London, and had much better dinners at that price, and would pay no more.

The waiter deſired to refer it to the preſident.—" I do not care a louſe for the preſident, ſays the ſtranger; all mankind are *equal*, and I inſiſt upon ' the rights of man;' and will not give up my unalienable liberty of getting a dinner, wherever I can meet with it."

The waiter urged, that the ſociety had agreed, and ordered a dinner at ſo much a head. The ſtranger ſaid, " *no body* of men could bind another to what he had not given his conſent." Beſides, an agreement made before dinner may be broken after dinner: a man may ſee reaſons, when his belly is full, which he could not ſee on an empty ſtomach.

This

This extraordinary doctrine being uttered with ſome emphaſis, the chaplain, who was an orthodox ſon of the church, ſaid, in a loud whiſper, that he fancied it was Dr. P----t--y in diſguiſe: "No, ſir, ſays the ſtranger, I am not Dr. P----t--y, I reſpect the Doctor as a philoſopher and a divine; he has made *free* enough with the ſecrets of nature, and with the *myſteries* of religion; but he does not come up to my ſtandard in politicks: my name is Thomas P—ne; and I do not care who knows it!"

"What buſineſs have you amongſt a company of taylors, then, cries one of them, and will not pay your reckoning?"

"Sir, I am a brother of the *thimble*; and a Staymaker by trade; which, ſurely, is ſuperior to a Taylor; as you all acknowledge the ſovereignty of your wives and miſtreſſes over their huſbands or keepers."

This rouſed the ſpirit of the whole fraternity; who, ſtarting up like the ſoldiers of Cadmus, inſtantaneouſly, each man with his arms a-kimbo declared, no woman in Chriſtendom ſhould rule *him*. The Preſident likewiſe, clapping on his Khevenhuller hat, and ſnatching up the ſtandard, ſaid, he would be glad to ſee the woman that ſhould *dare* to controul him: this was echoed by every man, from the top to the bottom of the table; and the tumult became ſo noiſy, that in ruſhed a whole body of Amazons; who, thinking their beloved ſpouſes had enjoyed their liberty and their jollity long enough, had come, as if by conſent, to the hotel, and each of them ſeizing upon her *lord* and *maſter*, dragged him off in triumph, and diſperſed the aſſembly.

ON THE

MORAL CHARACTERS

OF

THEOPHRASTUS.

THEOPHRASTUS's Moral Charaſters, mutilated as they are come down to us, are ſome of the moſt curious remains of antiquity. Having been written two thouſand years ſince, they are a proof that human nature was always the ſame; and that the ſame degree of civilization will produce the ſame ſtate of manners, the ſame vices and follies, in every age and in every country. Diſſimulation and flattery, impertinence and impudence, are the growth of every climate. The newſmonger of Theophraſtus is to be met with in our metropolis, and in almoſt every provincial town; but the peculiar prevalence of this character at Athens, where the author repreſents them as ſpending their whole time in the porticos, and other places of publick reſort, confirms St. Paul's account of the Athenians in his time; "that they employed themſelves in nothing "but in hearing and telling ſome new thing." So intent were theſe politicians, on getting a crowd about them in the publick baths,* to communicate their intelligence; that "their clothes were frequently ſtolen from them by ſharpers;" and, while they were taking towns and gaining victories, they were probably at a loſs for a dinner.

Some of theſe characters, however, are not ſufficiently diſcriminated, but might have been ranged under the ſame heads; as, thoſe upon flattery and *wheedling*, (as an old tranſlation calls it) thoſe upon garrulity and loquacity, and ſome few others.

As I have obſerved in many inſtances, where the idiom of the Greek language approaches nearer to the Engliſh than the Latin or any other of the dead language, a tranſlation nearly literal might beſt expreſs the ſenſe of the original, I have attempted one or two characters, to ſatisfy the curioſity of the mere Engliſh reader.

ON

* Like our Coffee-houſes.

GARRULITY.

GARRULITY, is a propenſity to be prating inceſſantly on unintereſting ſubjects. A garrulous man, or prating fellow, is one who, if he happens to ſit next to a mere ſtranger, begins with an encomium on his own wife. He then entertains him with the particulars of his laſt night's dream: he next recounts every diſh that he had for dinner the preceding day. In the progreſs of his volubility, he obſerves how much more wicked men are in this age than in the former: that corn was very cheap in the market to-day; and that there are a great number of ſtrangers in town: that ſoon after the feaſt of Bacchus,* the ſhips might ſafely put to ſea: that if it pleaſed God to ſend ſome rain, the fruits of the earth would come on finely: that he intends to plough up his fallow field next year; but that the times are hard, and that it is difficult for a man to live in the world.

He then tells you, that Damippus exhibited the largeſt torch at the myſteries of Ceres; and informs you the exact number of the columns in the theatre built

* The greater Bacchanalian feſtival, celebrated in ſpring.

built by Pericles. I took an emetick yesterday, he says; and pray what day of the month is it to-day?*

In short, if you have patience to listen to him, you will never get rid of him; but if you would avoid a fever, make your escape from such fellows with all possible speed, for there is no bearing with people, who have not sense to distinguish between seasons of business and of leisure.

Of DISTRUST;

OR,

A SUSPICIOUS TEMPER.

THIS suspicious temper inclines us to suspect every one of an intention to impose upon us. A man of this temper, if he sends his servant to market to buy provisions, will dispatch another servant, to enquire how much he paid for them. If he travels with a sum of money in his pocket, he will stop every half mile to reckon how much it is. As he lies in bed, he asks his wife

* He alludes to several other festivals, and exemplifies St. Paul's opinion of them. "Ye men of Athens! I perceive that in all things ye are too superstitious."

wife whether ſhe has ſhut the great cheſt, and locked the trunk carefully; and whether the bar was put to the outward-door? And, though ſhe aſſures him that all is ſafe, he nevertheleſs will leap out of his bed, and without his cloaths, and bare-footed, light a lamp, and go all round the houſe, and examine every particular; and even then can hardly compoſe himſelf to ſleep.

When he goes to receive the intereſt of thoſe who owe him money, he takes witneſſes with him, that they may not deny the debt for the future: if he ſends his coat to be ſcoured, he never enquires for the moſt ſkilful workman, but one that will give him the beſt ſecurity for returning it again: if a neighbour comes to borrow ſome drinking *glaſſes** of him, he is very unwilling to lend them; or if he does, he is never at reſt till he has got them returned: he bids his ſlave that attends him walk in his ſight before him, to prevent his running away: if a gentleman buys any thing of him, and bids him place it to his account; "No, ſir, pleaſe to lay down the money, for I ſhall not be at leiſure to ſend after it."

OF

* Εκπωματα.

OF

UNPLEASANT MANNERS;

OR,

TROUBLESOME FELLOWS.

THIS is a kind of intercourſe, though not abſolutely injurious, yet extremely irkſome and fatiguing. A troubleſome fellow is one who will go into your chamber, when you are juſt fallen to ſleep, and awake you, merely to have ſome idle converſation with him. And when a friend is going a voyage, and juſt ready to ſet ſail, he will go to him, and beg him to ſtay till they have taken a little walk together. He will take a child from its nurſe, chew ſome meat and feed it, dandle it in his arms, and talk nonſenſe to it; and, in the midſt of dinner, tells you that he took a doſe of hellebore, which operated powerfully upward and downwards;* and that after taking a little broth, he voided a great deal of black bile. He *frequently aſks*† his mother before company, what day ſhe brought him into the world? He tells you what fine cool water he has in his ciſtern; and that his garden produces great plenty of

* ἀνω και κάτω. † Δεινος, a terrible fellow.

of excellent and tender cabbages; and that his houſe is as open to all ſtrangers, as an inn upon the road; and when he has company, he introduces his paraſite as a facetious fellow, and during the entertainment, bids him exert himſelf and divert the company."

As the manners of the Athenians, at this period, were highly poliſhed, Theophraſtus muſt have taken many of theſe characters from the lower circles: he was turned of ninety (it is ſuppoſed) when he wrote them: he was the ſcholar and ſucceſſor of Ariſtotle, in his ſchool. Menander availed himſelf of theſe characters.

METRO-MANIA;

OR,

ON A RAGE FOR RHYMING.

" The graveſt bird that wings the ſky,
" His talents at a *ſong* will try."

ANONYM. (See the title-page.)

IN every civilized (and perhaps uncivilized) nation of the world, there has ſprung up once in an age, ſuppoſe, ſome exalted genius; who, conſcious of his own powers, has profeſſed himſelf a *prieſt* of the Muſes;* devoted himſelf to their ſervice, boldly laid claim to their inſpiration, and has been univerſally honoured with the reſpectable name of *poet*; ſuch were Homer, Virgil, Taſſo, Milton, and ſome few others.

There have likewiſe been, in every age, men of parts; who, making peotry their chief ſtudy, without aſpiring to the ſummit of Parnaſſus, have entertained and inſtructed

* Muſarum Sacerdos. HOR.

ſtructed mankind, by their didactick and moral poems; ſuch as Heſiod, Horace, Boileau, Dryden, Pope, and many others of that character. But there have been many more, particularly in our own country, who, miſtaking a ſtrong inclination for *genius*, have unhappily paid their court to the muſes: but, ſenſible at length of their own mediocrity of talents, have thought it neceſſary to make apologies for indulging ſo idle a propenſity; yet, by a ſtrange infatuation, perſevere in a practice which they affect to condemn.

Indeed, from what I have, even from my childhood, experienced in myſelf and obſerved in others; in the moſt illiterate as well as thoſe of the moſt improved underſtandings; this propenſity ſeems ſo general, that I am almoſt inclined to pronounce man "a *rhyming*, as well as a *reaſoning* animal." The rude efforts of the untaught multitude tend to prove, and the occaſional effuſions of more enlightened minds, to confirm, the juſtneſs of this definition. The chief difference between a man of ſenſe, and a coxcomb, in this reſpect, ſeems to conſiſt in the extent of their indulgence in this frivolous occupation. A man whoſe imagination prevails over his judgment, is apt to make rhyming his ſerious employment; while a ſenſible man makes it the amuſement only of a leiſure hour, and never ſuffers it to interfere with his more important purſuits.

Yet,

Yet, though we juſtly ridicule a mere rhymer, we may be thankful that we have been preſerved from a contagion, with which more or leſs, as I obſerved, ſome of the wiſeſt men in all ages have been infected: philoſophers, ſtateſmen, lawyers, and divines, have occaſionally felt ſymptoms of this epidemical diſeaſe.

We need not have recourſe to the remoter periods of Greece or Rome, to the examples of Solon, Plato, and even the wiſe Socrates: to thoſe of Scipio, Lelius, and Cicero: in a later æra, the amiable Pliny the conſul; who, beſides his high office, had ſo many more uſeful accompliſhments to value himſelf upon, ſpeaks with much ſelf-complacency of a volume of hendecaſyllables, which he had publiſhed, and which ſome Greeks, then reſiding at Rome, had ſet to muſick: though, if he has given us a fair ſpecimen of them, they were as bad as Tully's well-known jingle:

"O! *fortunatam natam*, me Conſule Romam!*

"How *happy happened* Rome to be,
"Bleſt with a Conſul thus like me!"

---

* Though Tully has been ridiculed for that (probably) extempore line; ſome people have thought, that, if he had cultivated his taſte for poetry, he would have made no bad figure in that branch. His poem on his countryman C. Marius was much admired by Atticus and other good judges. A middling orator might probably make a tolerable poet; but he had better exerciſe his lungs as an auctioneer, than in ſpouting his own heroics.

But our own country and more modern times, will furniſh us with ſufficient inſtances of the faſcinating charms of metre.

Amongſt the illiterate we may reckon John Bunyan; who, not contented with having produced his univerſally admired, original work of the Pilgrim's Progreſs, has exhibited his talent at rhyming, in a preface of five pages:

" Some ſaid, John, print it; others ſaid not ſo!
" Some ſaid, it might do good; others ſaid no!"

In the ſame rank of literature, though of much ſuperior poetical abilities, our own times ſupply us with examples without number.

But in the moſt highly cultivated underſtandings, this barren weed has occaſionally ſprung up in the midſt of more valuable productions.

Not to mention our Bolingbrokes, our Pulteneys, our Cheſterfields, and Nugents, and many others;* there is hardly a great man now living, but has in his youth, and perhaps in the zenith of his power and importance, ſported with the Muſes. Archbiſhops and biſhops,

* See Dodley's Miſcellanies, paſſim.

biſhops, ſtateſmen and lawyers; who have figured in the miniſtry, or preſided in the courts of judicature; many of whom, if it were decent or neceſſary, I could readily enumerate.*

Theſe reflections were ſuggeſted by reading the late philoſophical Dr. Berkenhout's letters to his ſon; in which, after ſome ſevere reflections on our publick ſchools and univerſities, (which however, by the way, the good Doctor ſhews to be undeſerved) and in the midſt of a moſt ſerious lecture on his ſon's moral and religious conduct, the Doctor concludes with inviting him to dinner, in a long epiſtle in rhyme, with the alliteration in which the reader will be diverted:

" To† *Trumpington tramping*, to dine with the Doctor,
" Which ſure you may do, without fear of the Proctor, &c.

But

* Sir W. Bl—kſtone, notwithſtanding the " Lawyer's farewell to his Muſe," (ſee Dodſley's Miſ.) could not forbear now and then ſome little dalliance with the enchanting nymph, when his admirable Commentaries had eſtabliſhed his fame, and ſecured him univerſal applauſe.

† The Doctor lived in Mr. Anſtey's houſe at Trumpington, near Cambridge; whom he compliments as the author of " The Bath Guide;" but forgets that his poetical is not the only valuable part of that gentleman's character.

But I do not produce these respectable examples, as an adequate excuse for my own offences in the same kind: nor is it a sufficient plea, that because a right reverend, or a right honourable personage, has in his youth written a few *good* verses, I should, in my old age, be scribbling so many bad ones. The only useful inference which I can draw from the premises, is to caution young people from indulging so unprofitable a pursuit; as an habit of rhyming, like any other habit, as drunkenness or fornication for instance, increases by indulgence; and though it may not bring us to the pillory, it will first or last, it is to be feared, bring us to shame. Indeed, if as Swift observes this tendency to rhyming be a morbid secretion from the brain, it may be as dangerous to check the humour too suddenly, as to stop up a defluxion or cold in the head by violent medicines; but let us at least attend to what Epectitus says of those that tell their dreams; which is applicable to those who write verses: "Never tell thy dreams, says that philosopher; for though thou mayst take a pleasure in *telling* them, another will take no pleasure in *hearing* them!"

"Nec lusisse pudet, sed non incidere ludum." Hor.

"Blush not in youth, to sport in rhyme,
"But pray, my friend, leave off in time." Anonym.

POSTCRIPT.

THIS Metro-mania is not peculiar to our own times or our own country: the learned Jeſuit Strada made the ſame complaint, in the 16th century, at Rome.

"Nullus hodiè mortaliûm aut naſcitur aut moritur; aut prœliatur aut ruſticatur; aut peregrè abit aut redit; aut *nubit*; aut eſt, aut non eſt; (nam etiam mortuis iſti canunt) cui illi non extemplò cudant epicedia, genethiaca; protreptica panegyrica; epithalamia, vaticinia; *propemptica*,* ſoterica; paræpetica; nænias, nugas.—Prolus. Academ.

"No mortal in this age is either born or dies; or *marries*; or goes to war, or goes into the country; or goes abroad, or returns home; or in ſhort, either exiſts or does not exiſt; (for even to the dead they ſing) for whom theſe rhymers do not immediately compoſe their birth-day odes; their elegies; their *epithalamiums*; their admonitory, and exhortatory, their panegyrical and prophetical rhymes; their congratulations and funeral ſongs; and trifles of every denomination."

* Complimentary wiſhes to a friend on his journey—we have no Engliſh word to expreſs it.

PART II.

POETICAL:

CONSISTING OF

A NEW TRANSLATION

OF

Holdſworth's Muſcipula,

AND

ORIGINAL PIECES.

PREFACE.

MR. HOLDSWORTH's *Muſcipula*, though ſo exquiſite a piece of humour in the original, yet depends ſo much on the ingenious application of expreſſions from the Claſſicks, that no tranſlation can do it juſtice. Dr. HOADLY's, in blank verſe, gives the ſenſe, but not the leaſt idea of the ſpirit and force of the original. Whether the following attempt will have better ſucceſs, it is impoſſible for me to judge. A man may pleaſe himſelf in humming a tune, yet afford no pleaſure to his company.

As I am myſelf a Welchman by my mother's ſide, and am poſſeſſed of a pedigree of the *Morgans'* family five yards long; and can prove my deſcent from a knight of King Arthur's round table; no one I truſt, will ſuſpect me of any diſrepectful intention, towards that ancient race of Britons, in an attempt to make the *Muſcipula* more extenſively known.

General reflections on bodies of men, on nations, or profeſſions, are univerſally condemned. But as for common-place jokes, a ſenſible man will join perhaps in the laugh, if the wit deſerve it; yet, with a conſcious ſuperiority, will pity the abſurd prejudices of thoſe that adopt them; who, however, are ſeldom actuated by any worſe paſſion than an ambition of being witty upon the moſt eaſy terms.

N. B. I have omitted a few lines, which deſcribe the ſtructure of the mouſe-trap: which, though expreſſed in elegant Latin, would make no figure in Engliſh; and, if the reader has *never ſeen* a mouſe-trap, he would have but a faint idea of it, from a poetical deſcription.

THE MUSCIPULA

OF

MR. HOLDSWORTH.

A NEW TRANSLATION.

THAT Britiſh Mountaineer, whoſe ſhrewd device
First forg'd coercive bonds for pilfering mice;*
Th' inſidious Trap's inextricable fate,
And all its various wiles, oh Muſe, relate!
And thou, great *Sminthian*† Phœbus, aid my ſong:
To thee, dread foe to mice! theſe lays belong,
And, from the Cambrian mountains, deign to chuſe
Another *Pindus*; while th' adventurous muſe

* Monticolam Britonem, qui primus *vincula* muri
Finxit, et ingenioſo occluſit carcere murem,
Lethaleſque dolos et inextricabila fatum,
Muſa refer ——— &c.

† So called from his deſtroying the mice, that infeſted that part of Phrygia. HOM.

Delights to ſport in tragi-comic verſe,
And fam'd exploits in humble ſtrains rehearſe.

Hoſtile to man, the mouſe, who long had reign'd,
By fear unaw'd, by danger unreſtrain'd;
Inur'd to rapine, his clandeſtine trade
Dauntleſs purſued, and direful havock made;
In every luſcious diſh he dipt his noſe,
Skipt to and fro, and ſported with his foes.
Nor doors, nor bolts, his ravages reſtrain,
Strong walls and pye-cruſt were oppos'd in vain;
A foe domeſtick, an unbidden gueſt,
The little thief intrudes at every feaſt.
He ate his way, where entrance was denied;
With unbought dainties by his tooth ſupplied.
But, while throughout the globe this peſt prevail'd,
CAMBRIA with ten-fold grief his thefts bewail'd.
She in her bowels nurs'd the dire diſeaſe,
For Cambria daily ſmelt of toaſted cheeſe.
And, not content to nibble, many a mouſe
Had here ſcoop'd out a comfortable houſe;
Here dwelt and batten'd, and ſecurely ſlept,
And undiſturb'd, his lawleſs revels kept.

With indignation fir'd, the Cambrian race
Ran wildly o'er their hills, from place to place:
While various ſtratagems their thoughts engage,
They fret; they ſtorm, their boſoms burn with rage;

For Cambria's ſons are ever prone to ire:
You'd ſwear, their ſouls,* with ſulphur ting'd, took fire.

As rage ſuggeſted, 'tis at length decreed,
Juſt vengeance muſt take place—the foe muſt bleed;
But how, or when? What project, who can find;
What wily ſnare, this cautious thief can bind?
Devoted Wales! The cat, though much thy friend,
Thy cheeſe, alas! no longer can defend:
Before the cavern's mouth, though night and day,
With look demure, ſhe watches for her prey;
With ſilent foot or, creeping, to ſurpriſe
The little caitiff: he for refuge flies
And ſits ſecurely in his winding dome,
Where cats of portly bulk can never come:
Nor dares peep out, or new excurſions try,
While murderous foes in treacherous ambuſh lie.

Thus, when great *Julius* had the world ſubdued,
And through the Britiſh iſle his foes purſued;
The Welch, if mice with Welchmen may compare,
Amidſt their rocks eſcaped the ſhocks of war;
Safe in their native bulwarks, they defy'd
The arms of Cæſar and the Roman pride,

* —— Credas animos *quoque* ſulphure tinctos.

That "quoque" is ſcurrilous; inſinuating that the Welch uſe brimſtone for ſome ſecret complaint.

Bravely they *fled* the well diſputed field;
Deſpair'd to conquer—yet diſdained to yield:
Hence his long pedigree the Cambrian boaſts,
Primæval language, and unconquer'd hoſts.

When thus the mouſe had long eſcaped the paw
Of fierce grimalkin; and the Cambrian ſaw
No hopes of ſuccour from his old ally,
More vigorous meaſures 'tis reſolv'd to try.

Where old Menevia,* on the diſtant ſhore,
Laments her ancient grandeur now no more,
Her walls demoliſh'd, and her mitre wrong'd,
A council is conven'd; when thither throng'd
Of aged ſires, and of Patricians proud,
And, ſteam'd with ſulphur, *an ignoble* crowd.
An ancient ſage, whoſe patriarchal beard,
By goats was envied—as by men rever'd,
Inveterate ſcurf incruſts his face and hands,
Conſpicuous, 'midſt the full aſſembly ſtands.
A *poſt* there was; and now, infirm with age,
Againſt the well-ſcrub'd *poſt* reclin'd the ſage;
And thus began:—deep from his aged throat,
With throttling ſound burſt forth the gutt'ral note.
"'Tis not for open war, that here we meet,
"But of a ſecret, pilfering foe, to treat:

---

* Now St. David's.

" 'Tis not his ſtrength or courage that we feel;
" He comes not boldly here to rob—but ſteal.
" No foreign enemy infeſts the land;
" But a more dangerous *inmate* we withſtand.
" How long, ye gods! ſhall this audacious mouſe,
" Still domineer, and pillage every houſe?
" But you, ye fathers, to whoſe guardian cares,
" Cambria looks up, in her diſtreſs'd affairs;
" Your ſage decrees our ſufferings muſt redreſs,
" And future ages ſhall your councils bleſs.
" Your patriot acts poſterity proclaim,
" And join with great Cadwallader's *your* name."

He ſpake; and, rais'd to the aſſembly's view,
Some mouldy fragments 'midſt the rabble threw,
The relicks of baſe theft: the ſight of theſe
Fir'd the brave Cambrians for their plunder'd cheeſe.
Now thirſt of vengeance, now the luſt of praiſe,
Ambitious thoughts in every boſom raiſe,
Unheard-of fates for mice each wight prepares,
Each head contrives inextricable ſnares.

Above the reſt, illuſtrious by his name,
But more by wit diſtinguiſh'd than by fame,
TAFFY, the glory of the Cambrian race,
Whoſe acts, unrivall'd, Britiſh annals grace:
The ſame a ſenator and blackſmith too;
Could make a florid ſpeech—or make a ſhoe.

He thus began; "If mice our cheeſe devour,
"Robb'd of their whole repaſt they ſtarve the poor;
"Nor will the rich behold, without remorſe,
"The want of cheeſe to crown their ſecond courſe.
"Since then nor cats nor courage aught avail,
"To quell this monſter ſince all efforts fail;
"The deep, mechanick powers ſhall now be tried:
"What *ſtrength* denies, by *art* ſhall be ſupplied.
"If force or fraud the enemy ſubdues,
"Who will enquire, what ſtratagems we uſe?"

Charm'd with his vaunting ſpeech, the liſt'ning throng
With fix'd attention on his accents hung:
They humm'd applauſe, with cheerful hopes inſpir'd;
But eager more to learn, their ſouls were fir'd,
And round the chief with wiſhful looks they ſtand,
And the whole proceſs of his ſcheme demand.
He ſcratch'd his head, for Cambrians wont to ſcratch,
Then thus proceeds the buſineſs to diſpatch;
But grinn'd a ghaſtly ſmile before he ſpoke,
And from his unlock'd jaws* theſe accents broke:
"Laſt night, repoſing from the toils of day,
"While ſtretch'd at eaſe, with wearied limbs, I lay,
"With ſleep profound my heavy eyes oppreſt,
"And all my faculties ſunk down to reſt;

* "Ora reſolvens talia verba refert."

" By ſteams of cheeſe, yet unconcocted, led,
" On which that night, as uſual, I had fed;
" Cloſe to my lips a mouſe the flavour draws,
" Who boldly enters my diſtended jaws;
" Thence ſliding down my throat, the thief, alas!
" By ſtealth crept through the ill-defended paſs.
" My laſt night's ſupper he attempts to eat,
" And with crude lumps of cheeſe again retreat:
" Rous'd from my ſleep, within my teeth I ſnapp'd,
" And in cloſe bonds the ſtruggling thief entrapp'd.
" Indignant, his eſcape he tries in vain,
" Held in cloſe durance by the biting chain.
" Thus, by experience taught, with joy I found
" That mice, like men, in fetters might be bound;
" And, as my teeth the captive mouſe had preſs'd,
" Some new machine, like that, my thoughts ſuggeſt.
" Cloſe meditation ſhall my ſcheme befriend;
" And, by my ſkill, ſhall our misfortunes end.

" By what myſterious laws, what ſecret chain
" Of cauſes ſtrange, does heav'n the world ſuſtain!
" The mouſe himſelf an antidote has taught
" To all the miſchiefs which himſelf has wrought.
" Nor would you ſure, to learn from foes, diſdain,
" Nor uſeful knowledge ev'n from mice to gain."

Thus ſpake the chief: and to his home withdrew,
The crowd applaud him, and with prayers purſue

The flattering aſpect of his counſels bleſs,
And wiſh his toils their merited ſucceſs.

Then to their houſes all with ſpeed retire,
And tell of theſe glad tidings round their fire;
What bleſſings were by Taffy's hands decreed:
And while with heaven their vows for Taffy plead;
The cats, prophetic of bleſt times to come,
With glee unuſual ſported round the room:
Nay, if 'tis true, as it recorded ſtands,
The cheeſe-curds danc'd beneath the matron's hands.

Taffy, meanwhile, who ſoft repoſe denies,
To head or hand his uſeful labour plies:
By Pallas, in each curious ſcience ſkill'd,
With art divine the mouſe-trap taught to build;
In form complete, as yet to mortals new,
The tragi-comic ſtructure roſe to view!*

Thus all things finiſh'd Taffy, now prepares
For hapleſs mice inevitable ſnares.
The fatal hook ſuſpends the treacherous bait,
And ev'n their food by Taffy's arm'd with fate.
To tempt more widely and to charm the more,
He adds new ſtrength to cheeſe—ſo ſtrong before:

* The proceſs of making a mouſe-trap here omitted.

For ſtill to make the attractive flavour higher,
He toaſts the ſavoury morſel at the fire.

And now approach'd the memorable night,
(His work complete) when Taffy with delight
His weary limbs was ſolacing in bed;
His truſty mouſe-trap ſtation'd at his head,
Sweet ſleep indulg'd. The mice, a ſaucy crew,
Leap forth, as uſual, and their pranks renew.
But while they ſport beneath night's ſilent ſhade,
One more ſagacious, mindful of his trade;
A mouſe of rank; but, born the gods his foes,
Drawn by the grateful ſcent that reach'd his noſe;
To th' hoſtile trap, in evil hour, he hies,
When lo! admiſſion the cloſe grate denies.
Provok'd at this repulſe, with rage he burns;
The wir'd machine on every ſide by turns
With wrinkled noſe explores—and with much pains
Th' irremeable paſs at length he gains.
The thoughtleſs mouſe devours the deadly bait,
" Feaſts on his ruin, and enjoys his fate."

Rous'd by the noiſe; which, near his pillow laid,
The trap, by dropping of its portal made;
Prop'd on his elbow, Taffy rais'd his head,
Then leap'd with joy triumphant from his bed,
Eager to learn what gueſt approach'd his houſe;
When lo! appears the little angry mouſe.

With head, with foot, he fights, and vents his rage,
And, with fell tooth attacks the wiry cage.
Thus rages in his toils, and ſtrives in vain,
The Marſian boar to break his hempen chain,
The waving net his effort cloſer draws,
Sport to the dogs he raves, and from his jaws
The plenteous foam he daſhes on the ſand,
While on his back erect the briſtles ſtand.

Now roſe the morn:—The joyful news to hear
Down from their rocks th' impatient crowds appear.
For lo! the aſs, or ancient bards have lied,
His gravity and ſloth now laid aſide,
The mountain climbs, more nimble than a goat,
And like an herald, from his ruſty throat,
Thee, Taffy, thrice with honour due he names,
And braying thrice the publick joy proclaims.

The owl, the Cambrian envoy, too, 'tis ſaid,
Through all her towns the fatal news convey'd.
All night ſhe wanders;—and with mournful ſhriek
Againſt their windows daſh'd her ominous beak,
And through each ſtreet proclaim'd to every houſe,
The fates impending o'er the hapleſs mouſe.
" The mountains* now in labour" from their ſides,
Their ſons in crowds, deſcend like ruſhing tides:

* See the 7th book of the Æneid, 640, for this and many of the imitations.

From Pembroke and Mervinia* many a clown,
From craggy hills, elate with joy, ran down:
And Bangor's ſons, whoſe brow the mitre cown'd;
And, through the world for Merlin's birth renown'd,
Old Maridunum:† whom thy fertile vale,
Glamorgan feeds: or who, on cheeſe regale,
And Vaga's‡ waters drink, romantick ſtream!
With ſturdy ſwains that from Montgomery came.

Then Taffy thus, ſurrounded by the crowd,
His captive foe inſults, with accents proud:
" 'Tis vain to ſtruggle, thief! thy doom's decreed;
" That thou, firſt victim! on my altar bleed.
" Dream not of flight; for know, thy hope is vain;
" Mark of thy guilt, thy blood this trap ſhall ſtain.
" Whoe'er its entrance tempts with evil ſtars,
" Shall ne'er repaſs th' inexorable bars:
" Thou for thy wicked deeds, nor hope reprieve,
" Thy priſon and thy life at once ſhalt leave."
Scarce had he ſpoke; when lo! th' inſidious cat
Leap'd from the cottage-thatch, where oft ſhe ſat
Luxurious baſking in the ſunny ray—
With limbs extended, all a ſummer's day.

The captive ſpied his foe; his prick'd-up ears,
And gibbous, briſtling back, expreſs'd his fears.

* Merioneth. † Carmarthen. ‡ The Wye.

He watch'd the cat's approach; and now no more
Attempts, though open, the ſuſpended door.
Back to the priſon's utmoſt bound he flies,
Which all his hopes of ſafety now ſupplies:
With hooked claws he graps his wiry chains,
And with tenacious feet a while remains;
Thence ſhaken off, he drops, prepar'd for flight,
When now the cat, more rapid than the light,
Flies on her prey: whom ſtruggling to get free,
Her cloſe embraces hug; which ill agree
With her fell purpoſe: for with ſavage art,
And cruel ſport, the tyrant plays her part:
No reſpite grants; her ſinuous tail ſhe plies,
Expreſſive of her joy; now prone ſhe lies,
Watching the mouſe intent: with harmleſs claw
She ſtrokes his neck, or pats him with her paw;
With wanton ſallies then aloft ſhe ſprings,
While to the earth the trembling victim clings:
Eager to tear him, with feign'd love ſhe courts,
And with her prey tyrannically ſports.

With trifling tir'd, impatient of delay,
Grimalkin whets her tuſks; and o'er her prey,
Like a young lion growls: then, dropping gore,
His quivering limbs and breathing entrails tore.
The caitiff's blood, when now the ruſticks ken'd,
With joyful ſhouts the ambient air they rend:

Echo, that dwells in Cambria's cloſe retreats,
Well pleas'd herſelf the joyful ſhouts repeats;
The ſhouts aſcend Plinlimmon's lofty height,
Brechin and Snowdon in th' applauſe unite.
The neighbouring ſtars, and Cambria's utmoſt bounds,
And *Offa's dyke, with clamorous joy reſounds.

But, Taffy, thou for ages ſhalt ſurvive,
Thy Trap preſerve thy glorious name alive;
Ev'n now the Cambrian, each revolving year,
Thy merit celebrates with rural cheer,
Of Cambria's honour ſav'd with rapture ſpeaks,
And decks his feſtive brow with fragrant leeks.

* If this be an anti-climax—the original is accountable for it.

ORIGINAL PIECES.

ADVERTISEMENT.

MANY of the following Rhymes were intended to express the Author's ſenſe of unmerited civilities, for which it was not in his power to make any other return: if the reader ſhould chuſe to impute them to adulation or vanity, inſtead of gratitude, the author can only ſay, that he is not conſcious of any ſuch motives.

THE LAMENTATION OF AN INVETERATE RHYMER.

IN Life's campaign, amidſt the battle's rage,
Where fevers, palſies, gouts, and—quacks, engage;
When I, a puny mortal! ſtill remain,
While thouſands fall around me on the plain;
Have almoſt brav'd it threeſcore years and ten,
The age allotted to the ſons of men:
When anxious thus I wait heaven's awful doom,
Stand trembling o'er the horrors of the tomb;
Shall I the moments waſte, inſtead of pray'r,
In jingling rhymes and carolling the fair?
Forgetting, I no longer am a boy,
Shall *childiſh* bawbles ſtill the *man* employ?
What penance for ſuch trifling can atone?
I feel, and, ah! with ſhame my folly own.
But ſome ſtrange charm by turns my boſom fires,
Or friendſhip's call with vanity conſpires;

Some ſmiling nymph enjoins her rhyming taſks:
Some friend an epilogue or prologue aſks;
And, though I vow and promiſe, o'er and o'er,
To grow more ſerious and tranſgreſs no more;
I find my ſtrongeſt reſolutions vain:
I write, repent, reſolve, and write again.

But, ſince ſuch rhymes demand no vig'rous powers,
And juſt amuſe the idleſt of my hours;
When rules of health due exerciſe require,
Or rains confine me to my parlour fire;
When deaf my ears, and eyes refreſhment need,
Debarr'd ſweet converſe, and forbid to read;
From ſerious buſineſs, from intruſion free,
(Though age and youthful frolicks ill agree)
Then fancy, leagu'd with cuſtom, ſtill invades,
And tempts to wanton with th' Aonian maids;
Forgot awhile life's more important cares,
Again I'm caught in their ſeducing ſnares.

With gloom oppreſs'd, whene'er the reſtleſs mind
Attempts in ſprightlier ſcenes relief to find;
When airy viſions thus my thoughts engage,
I feel no more th' infirmities of age;
Diſpell'd by momentary gleams of joy,
Nor anxious fears nor fancied ills annoy:
Imagination youthful days renews,
And gilds with orient beams life's evening views.

Yet though these toys at intervals intrude,
They ne'er due thoughts of future hopes exclude.
Awhile I listen to these sportive strains;
But reason still, I trust, my sovereign reigns.
Though in my breast amusement claims its part,
I'm yet "a sad, good Christian at the heart:"
To virtue and to piety a friend,
Sing on the road—yet mindful of its end.

1786.

PHILOKALUS;

OR,

A PLEA FOR

UNSEASONABLE GALLANTRY.

OFT' by the ladies I am told,
(What long I've known) that I grow old;
And ought not thus, at ſixty-ſix,
With giddy, giggling girls to mix:
That ev'n my compliments but teaze them,
Though vainly I attempt to pleaſe them.

But, Chloe, not to make you proud,
The gilding of yon evening cloud,
Or luſtre of the orient ſun,
Has oft your brilliant charms outſhone.
And, lo! where'er I turn my eyes,
Enchanting objects round me riſe:
All which were made for our delight;
And which it were a ſin to ſlight.

If beauties of inferior kind,
Thus charm, to your's can I be blind.

Know then, I love each living creature!
Each pleaſing form of art or nature:
Ev'n lifeleſs things enamour'd view,
(Not with that fondneſs I do you)
I love a well-proportion'd column;
A well-carv'd buſt; a well-bound volume:
Each maſter-piece of every art
Claims a due portion in my heart:
Nay more, from charms which all admire,
My thoughts to heaven itſelf aſpire;
Smit with *your* beauties, lovely maid!
I ſtill want ſuch—as ne'er will fade.
Amidſt my cramps and other ſtrange ills,
I am eager to converſe with angels;
Such angels, as great Milton drew,
More friendly—not more fair—than you.

With love extenſive I embrace
The feather'd or unfeather'd race;
A peacock I have often ſeen
More charming than Burke's* captive Queen.

---

* Queen of France, whoſe perſon Mr. Burke ſpeaks of with deſerved enthuſiaſm.

With rapture I behold a lamb
Sporting around its anxious dam:
Nay, ſuch my love for harmleſs creatures,
That you yourſelf, with thoſe fine features,
With gauze your neck, with plumes your head dreſt,
Are rivall'd by a Robin-red-breaſt.

To call it *love* indeed's the faſhion;
Though oft with me 'tis pure compaſſion:
'Tis *pity* for their helpleſs ſtate,
That not a reptile I can hate;
But, as with pleaſure I behold
The inſect, ſtreak'd with mimick gold,
I, as my fellow-creature, greet
The ſnail, that crawls beneath my feet.

Thus, Chloe, ev'n my love for you
Has nothing ſelfiſh in its view:
I love each rural nymph I ſee;
But don't expect them to love me.
For you, with youthful ardour burn;
But dare not hope for a return:
No: trouble not your head about me,
But do not ridicule and flout me.

I love my ſpaniel and my pointer,
More than fair ——— or her jointure;

Though do not wiſh them to requite me,
But only—not to ſnarl, or bite me.

Ah! do not therefore call me fool,
Nor ſend me to Moorfields* to ſchool,
Becauſe I fondly gaze on you,
As every mortal man muſt do,
With admiration and delight,
Who is not void of taſte—or ſight.

* Bedlam.

DO YOUR OWN BUSINESS!

THE LARK

AND

HER YOUNG ONES.

A FABLE,

From A. GELLIUS.

NE QUID AB AMICO EXPECTES QUOD TUTE AGERE POSSIS.

WHEN autumn now had deck'd the plain
With waving crops of golden grain,
To crown the anxious farmer's care,
And for their harveſt all prepare:
A Lark had left her infant brood,
To range the fields in queſt of food;
But charg'd them, as conceal'd they lay,
(If chance the farmer came that way)
To liſten what they heard him mention,
That might diſcover his intention,

How ſoon he meant to cut his wheat,
That they might thence in time retreat.
Having her caution thus expreſs'd,
She left them cuddling in their neſt—
But, when return'd, in wild affright
They begg'd her to remove that night:
For that the farmer told his ſon,
'Twas time their harveſt was begun;
And that he'd call his *neighbours* in,
And the next morning would begin.

If that be all, the mother ſaid,
We need not yet be much afraid:
He that depends upon his neighbour,
Will find him ſparing of his labour.
People are ſlow to ſerve their friends,
Unleſs it anſwers their own ends.

The lark next morning does the ſame,
Again the careful farmer came;
And, ſince his *neighbours* thus had us'd him,
And ſo unhandſomely refus'd him;
Piqu'd as he was, he bids his ſon
Ride o'er and aſk his uncle John,
And couſin George, and couſin Tom:
For they, he ſaid, would gladly come.

The young ones now inform'd the mother,
The farmer had engag'd his *brother*;

And had resolv'd, without delay,
To cut his corn the following day.

The mother bade them *yet* not fear:
" Relations, should they be sincere,
Have seldom been so punctual known
In others' business, as their own."

Accordingly, their loving cousins
Found out excuses by the dozens:
The uncle was not very well,
And when he should be, could not tell.
Their cousin George he could not spare;
And Tom was gone to Banbury fair.
Yet, he was sorry to refuse him;
But hoped his brother would excuse him.

The farmer, now reduced to straights,
No longer for assistance waits;
More disappointments would not bear,
But bids his son two hooks prepare;
And they themselves, the following morn,
Would certainly cut down their corn.

When this the trembling inmates hear,
They seriously began to fear
Their threats would now effectual prove,
And instantly prepar'd to move.

He that on neighbours or on friends
To do his work too much depends,
In ſpite of compliments repeated,
Will find his hopes too oft defeated.
If you would have your buſineſs done—
" Rely upon yourſelf alone."

CHOOSE

FOR

YOURSELF!

WHATE'ER philofophers may chatter;
Who know but little of the matter;
The greateft comforts of our life,
Are a good horfe—and a good wife:
One for domeftick confolation,
And one for health and recreation.
Be cautious then, but not too nice;
Nor liften to each fool's advice:
Nor, guided by the publick voice,
But your own reafon, make your choice.

My horfe was old and broken-winded,
Yet this myfelf I hardly minded;
But by my neighbours I was told,
That when a horfe grows ftiff and old,
If urg'd to fpeed—'tis ten to one
He trips and throws his rider down.

I liſten'd then to their advice,
And bought a colt—at no ſmall price:
A ſtately ſteed, that on the road
Would proudly prance beneath his load.
But this Bucephalus, again,
Put my young family in pain;
Who cordially expreſs'd their fears,
That I, a man advanced in years,
Regardleſs of my own *dear** neck,
Should undertake a colt to break.
You are too wiſe, dear ſir, I know
To hazard thus your life for ſhow;
Riſk then no ſubject for remorſe,
But part with this unruly horſe!

I next a pony would have bought,
An uſeful ſcrub: but here 'twas thought
(Such is my ſon's and daughter's pride)
It was too mean for me to ride.
Dear ſir! ſaid they, it is not fit
For you to mount this paltry tit:
It were as well almoſt, alas!
To ride, like Balaam, on an aſs.

Again, to various ſyſtems yielding,
I bought a ſtrong, ſtout, ſtumping gelding:

---

* φίλον ἦτορ. Hom.

Affured he'd neither trip nor ftart;
Would carry me—or draw a cart.
But vain were all my irkfome labours,
This clumfy beaft quite *fhock'd* my neighbours;
Who ftill would have me, as before,
At buying, try my hand once more.

One offer'd me a *pretty* mare,
Juft bought, he faid, at Briftol fair;
And then my landlord at the Bell
Had a young galloway to fell:
He'd travel fifty miles a-day—
" But try him, fir, before you pay."
He would not willingly have fold him,
But fomebody, he faid, had told him,
How much, forfooth, I was diftrefs'd!
And earneftly the matter prefs'd:
So, willing to do *me* a *favour*,
He wifh'd, he faid, that I might have her.
" Well, landlord, you're *an honeft* man,
I'll pleafe my neighbours if I can;
I'm not a judge, you know, myfelf,
I'll truft to you—here take the pelf—"
The purchafe made, I now grew wife—
Man John, faid I, how are his eyes?
Oh! fir, not blind, you need not fear it,
I mean not yet—though very near it.

Thus then on every ſide *put to't*,
I vow'd at laſt, I'd walk on foot:
For 'tis in vain, alas! I find,
To think of pleaſing all mankind.

'Tis thus in chuſing of a horſe;
In chuſing of a wife—'tis worſe.
Handſome or homely; young or old;
Chaſte or unchaſte; a wit; a ſcold;
Howe'er ſhe proves, how vain your labour
To pleaſe each prying, buſy neighbour!
Then pleaſe yourſelf; or elſe for life
Give up that uſeful thing—a wife.

☞ *The following Jeu d'Esprit found its way lately into a morning paper, and was there said to have been written by Dr. Sam. Johnson, while at breakfast with a lady, to shew her the facility with which compositions of this kind might be produced. From the subject, this anecdote is not very probable; neither has Mrs. Piozzi, or Mr. Boswell, mentioned any thing like it.*

SUNDAY SCHOOLS.

A PASTORAL.

TOM AND NANCY.

WHEN now the ſun had uſher'd in the morn,
And glittering dew-drops hung on every thorn;
Beneath the ſhadow of a ſpreading beech,
Tom lean'd, and Nancy ſate upon her breech.
Their bleating lambkins wander'd down the vale,
While Nancy liſten'd to the ſhepherd's tale:
Their faithful dog lay ſleeping by their ſide,
When Tom began, and Nancy thus replied.

TOM.

Believe me, Nancy, I'd a ſong indite
To chaunt thy praiſes, but—I cannot write.

NANCY.

With thee, dear Tom, I'll range the flowery mead;
But *write* no ſong; for ah!—I cannot read.

TOM.

Well, then: we'll love from day-light till 'tis dark,
And leave ſuch learning to the pariſh-clerk.

NANCY.

Or ev'n the parſon's maid might do as well;
For ſhe's a *ſcholard*, and can write and ſpell.

TOM.

d thou can'ſt knit and ſpin, and that is better;
And I can work, tho' I don't know one letter.

NANCY.

Oh, Tom! that we had learnt (when we were young)
Our *cat-i-kays*, our *prayers*, and *vulgar tongue!*

TOM.

Well, now each child may learn in Sunday Schools;
And little John will make *us* look like fools.

NANCY.

God bleſs 'Squire Raikes! who firſt theſe ſchools did found;
To which our gentry now give many a pound.

TOM.

Now boys and girls are taught to read and ſing,
And ſay their prayers, and pray for church and king.

NANCY.

Now neat and clean the boys and girls we meet;
Not running wild and ragged through the ſtreet.

TOM.

Then let us go to church, each Sunday night,
And hear them ſing *ſol-fa* with all their might.

NANCY.

We'll go; and tho' I cannot ſing the beſt,
My voice, ſo ſhrill, ſhall ſqueak amongſt the reſt.

TOM.

But lo! our ſheep quite out of ſight are got,
And now the mounting ſun ſhines plaguy hot.

NANCY.

Then you drive up your flock; and I'll go home,
And boil the pot, and ſpin till you are come.

Exeunt.

ON THE

DEATH OF

MR. HOWARD,

THE PHILANTHROPIST.

BORN to relieve the mis'ries of mankind,
Infenfible of toil, to danger blind;
Thro' diftant realms, while How'rd with zeal purfues,
And executes his philanthropick views;
Boldly defcends, when human fufferings call,
Where damps annoy or poifonous reptiles crawl;
His friends (nor lefs the friends of th' human race)
Thus check'd their colleague's rafhnefs in the chace:
" Why eager thus unequal war to wage,
" Where peftilence and death refiftlefs rage?
" Each captive wretch, and object of diftrefs,
" Nay, duty pleads thy ardour to reprefs.
" Thy life, more precious than of lords or kings,
" Life, health, and happinefs, to thoufands brings.
" Be not too bold, attend difcretion's call;
" Nor rifk for *one* the life that's due to *all*.

Stranger to fear, all danger he defied:
With temperance arm'd, and Providence his guide.
But angels, charm'd ſuch godlike acts to ſee,
Forgot awhile their guardian cares for thee.
Contagion then, whoſe powers had been ſuſpended,
Reſum'd its force, and, ah! thy work was ended:
Anxious for all, but for himſelf alone;
To ſave a ſtranger's* life, he loſt his own.
Oh! had he learnt the caution of a coward,
The world had ſtill been happy in their Howard.

---

* A young lady in a peſtilential fever.

AN HERO IN HUMBLE LIFE.

A TRIBUTE TO

THE MEMORY OF

MR. THOMAS UNDERWOOD,

Who loſt his Life to ſave a Fellow-ſervant from the Fire, at Cumberwell-houſe, Wilts, Dec. 8, 1790.

OF Heroes old, for ſlaughter'd foes renown'd;
Of kings, for vanquiſh'd realms with laurels crown'd;
Or patriots, in their country's cauſe who fell,
Let Grecian bards, or Roman annals tell.
To gain a victory Codrus *ſought* his death,
And Curtius in the gulph reſign'd his breath:
Illuſtrious be their acts, and juſt their fame,
They gain'd—'twas what they ſought—a deathleſs name.

Behold! a youth, untutor'd in the laws
Of Glory's ſchool, nor led by vain applauſe;

Yet, taught by mere humanity, exceeds
In ſolid glory all their boaſted deeds;
Eſcap'd from death, undaunted he returns,
While yet the fire in all its fury burns;
With ſuppliant cries, for lo! an helpleſs maid
Amidſt the burning manſion ſues for aid:
Boldly he ruſh'd, and ſav'd her in his arms—
But ah! another wretch his fears alarms.
In flames involv'd the trembling victim ſtands,
To heaven in wild deſpair ſhe lifts her hands:
By pure compaſſion, not with glory fir'd,
Again he ruſh'd—but in th' attempt expir'd.
Ye angels! o'er the deed who wond'ring ſtood,
Receive his ſpirit to your bleſt abode:
Ye Britiſh dames, protect the pregnant* wife,
For in *your* cauſe the huſband loſt his life.

---

* Big with her ſecond child.

ON THE

KING's RECOVERY.

10th MARCH, 1789.

IF o'er the ſun, at early day,
While mortals hail his cheering ray,
And nature ſmiles in vernal bloom,
Some cloud extends its tranſient gloom;
Through all the grove dull ſilence reigns,
And mirth and joy forſake the plains.

But ſoon diſpers'd the vapours fly,
Chas'd by the regent of the ſky;
The turbid air his beams refine,
And with their wonted luſtre ſhine.

Thus late BRITANNIA's happy iſle
Saw peace reſtor'd, and all things ſmile:
Beneath her much-lov'd monarch's reign,
Mirth revell'd o'er the wide domain:
Even rival factions only ſtrove
To expreſs their gratitude and love.

But ſee! a ſudden ſore diſeaſe
Our ſovereign's mental functions ſeize;
Whoſe dire effects at once oppreſs
The ſource of publick happineſs.

Then ſadneſs mark'd each face with grief,
Nor med'cine's ſelf affords relief;
Till heaven, in pity to our land,
Propitious ſent a lenient* hand;
Its aid with ardent prayers implor'd,
To health th' afflicted king reſtor'd.

Now rapture fills th' exulting iſle,
Again all nature ſeems to ſmile:
All parties join'd, one voice employ,
To teſtify the publick joy.

Our monarch heal'd is lov'd the more—
We felt but half his worth before.
His danger only ſerves to prove
Heaven's bounty, and his people's love.

---

* Dr. Willis.

WRITTEN IN

THE PAVILION,

In the LAUREL-GROVE,

At BURTON PYNSENT,

JULY 1786.

IMPROMPTU.

THE British flag, triumphantly display'd,
Throughout the world great Chatham's fame convey'd:
Our sinking credit, and our funds restor'd,
An equal triumph to young Pitt afford.
The sire, the victor's *laurel* justly won:
Let then an ***oaken* crown reward the *son.*

* Or civick crown formed of oak leaves, " ob cives servatos."

A

WINTER-DAY's JOURNEY;

OR,

THE STAGE OF LIFE!

WRITTEN AT AN INN, 1787.

AT early dawn, fresh rising with the sun,
With spirits gay, my journey I begun:
Thro' rough and smooth, 'midst sunshine, rain or snow,
O'er hill and dale, full merrily I go.

At noon I halt, refresh my weary steed;
Recruit my strength; then cheerfully proceed.
But soon I feel the tedious length of way,
My spirits waning with the closing day.
Now night succeeds; fatigu'd and listless grown,
I still jog on, all cheerless and alone:
I wish for rest; though yet no rest can find,
For many a tedious mile is still behind.
But ah! at length I spy the friendly light
Of a warm inn dispel the gloom of night:

Pleas'd I dismount, become a welcome guest,
Secure a well-warm'd bed—and sink to rest.

Yet, while my languid frame its strength renews,
My active fancy still her flight pursues;
The day's adventures traces o'er again,
Enjoys the pleasure, and forgets the pain.

In youth's fair season, thus alert and gay,
Our stage begins, and sunshine all the way:
Hope plans a life of never-ceasing joy;
No share of bliss our appetite can cloy:
To manhood grown, we yet behold awhile
The flattering world, with varying lustre, smile:
To-day, though disappointment cloud the scene,
To-morrow yields a prospect more serene;
Pleasure and pain alternately prevail,
Yet hope in pleasure's favour turns the scale:
But soon, alas! the fond delusion's o'er,
Dull cares succeed, and pleasure is no more.
The evil days approach, and naught remains,
But gloomy cares, infirmities and pains;
No further prospect now the wretch can have
Of joy, of ease, but in the friendly grave;
There let me flee, bid all my troubles cease,
There rest my weary limbs—and sleep in peace.
While, wing'd with hope my frailties are forgiven,
The soul, redeem'd from death, shall mount to heaven.

A

SUMMER-DAY's PLEASURE,

AT

C——Y, NEAR BATH.

DEEP in a vale, 'midſt pendant woods,
And verdant meads, and winding floods;
Sequeſter'd from that buſy ſcene
Of noiſe and ſhow—which nothing mean;
There ſtands a ſweet Palladian pile,
A manſion in the chaſteſt ſtyle;
Such as of old, full many a dome
Adorn'd the environs of Rome.

This, as his journey he purſues,
The traveller at a diſtance* views;
And, though impatient to proceed,
Charm'd with the landſcape, checks his ſteed;

L

---

* From the Wells road.

With rapture cries, nor deems amiſs,
" There ſurely is the ſeat of bliſs."
And happy he! of taſte poſſeſs'd,
Who hither comes a favour'd gueſt:
Complete within we all things find,
Taſte, elegance, and ſplendour, join'd.
Proportion'd rooms, where every art
Of ornament ſupplies its part.

A table furniſhes the treat,
Deck'd with ſuch food as folks can eat;
Superb indeed, but not profuſe,
Intended leſs for ſhow than uſe;
And though perhaps you eat on plate,
'Tis for convenience, not for ſtate:
For, ſpite of faſhion, I alledge,
That china ſets one's teeth on edge.
At perfect liberty and eaſe,
You ſay and do juſt what you pleaſe;
Within this hoſpitable dome,
Ev'n ſtrangers find themſelves at home.

What ſecret charm then ſhall we ſay,
Thus gilds our moments at C**b*h*y?
What ſpell inviſible pervades,
And animates theſe rural ſhades?
What genius o'er the place preſides,
Whoſe influence every movement guides?

The worthy owners' head and heart,
Their kind attentions ſtill impart;
And each politely condeſcends,
To treat you not as gueſts, but friends.
To *them* 'tis happineſs ſincere,
To ſee *you* happy whilſt you're here.
But fleeting hours glide on too ſoon,
And night, alas! ſucceeds to noon.
Too ſhort we find the ſummer's day,
When evening ſummons us away:
'Tis parting only gives us pain,
We part—yet long to meet again—
But hope not to engroſs thoſe hearts,
Where friends unnumber'd claim their parts.

WRITTEN UNDER

A BEAUTIFUL YOUNG OAK,

At H——, SOMERSET,

(The Seat of the late Col. B——.)

AT early morn, when oft I ſauntering rove,
And ſeek thy ſhade, fair Regent of the grove;
Or at thy root, where Laura deigns to twine
The woodbine round thy trunk, at eve recline;
Diſpell'd awhile the cloud of gloomy cares,
Which 'midſt his brighteſt days each mortal ſhares;
I pleas'd reflect on many a friendly proof
Of kindneſs, from yon' hoſpitable roof;
Where dwell politeneſs, elegance, and eaſe,
Minds fraught with equal *power* and *will* to pleaſe:
Where, ev'n to luxury, each favour'd gueſt
His appetite may pleaſe, his fancy* feaſt.

But though theſe ſcenes, where calmly thus I ſit,
I ſoon, alas! reluctantly muſt quit:

* With pictures, the production of the worthy owner's pencil.

Go hence forlorn, and ah! perhaps deplore
Theſe happy days, which *may** return no more;
Nay, all my ſublunary joys be paſt,
What ages are *thy* beauties form'd to laſt:
What various ſeaſons art *thou* doom'd to ſee,
What nymphs and ſwains ſhall make their moan to thee!
What idle bards with rapture haunt the vale,
And to the liſtening dryads tell their tale!

Ah! if, in future times, ſome thriftleſs heir,
By want impell'd, thoſe dryads ſhould not ſpare,†
Theſe ſylvan gods, with impious hand invade,
And rudely violate this awful ſhade;
O! tell the wretch, the curſe of every muſe,
And every child of taſte, ſuch deeds purſues.
Tell him! that he, unſhelter'd, in his turn,
Shall ſtarve in winter, and in ſummer burn.
That, like the blaſted oak, himſelf ſhall rot,
And die unſung, unpitied, and forgot.

If, with each tree, a dryad feel the ſtroke,
'Tis *murder*, ſure, to fell a ſtately oak:
Each grove is *ſacred*, taint not then thy mind
With guilt of ſacrilege and murder join'd.

May 29th, 1789.

* Ah nimis ex vero. Ov.

† There is no danger of ſuch an event, under the preſent worthy poſſeſſor.

A DIGNIFIED RETREAT.

WRITTEN AT

B**T*N-P*NSENT.

June 1789.

WHERE B-rt-n groves, with lofty ſtructures grac'd,
Proclaim great Chatham's merits*—and his taſte;
Who, on the nobleſt plans of ſtate employ'd,
Amidſt theſe ſhades domeſtick ſweets enjoy'd:
Till ſpent with patriot toils he ſunk to reſt,
With all his weeping country's wiſhes bleſt:
Hither, though long in poliſh'd courts admir'd,
The partner of his cares has now retir'd.
By friendſhip's aid, in widow'd ſtate, relieves
The loſs of that lov'd man for whom ſhe grieves;
For whom through life her grief might juſtly laſt,
Fed by remembrance of their pleaſures paſt.

Yet time perhaps the mournful gloom might chaſe,
And brighter thoughts inſenſibly take place;

* The reward of his patriotick conduct.

While on the marble urn,* ſhe 'midſt the grove
Records the bliſs of chaſte, connubial love;
Or, in the learned page finds that relief,
Which ſage and holy men preſcribe for grief.

But ah! again (ſo heaven, alas! decreed)
For lovely Eliot's† death her wounds muſt bleed:
A huſband's joy! a mother's darling pride!
In bloom of youth the lovely Eliot died.

Yet to her weeping friends, indulgent Heav'n
A tranſcript of the parent's charms has given:
In virtue's ſhade the tender plant to rear,
Chatham again exerts a mother's care:
Pleas'd in the lovely offspring's docile mind,
The parent's virtues with her charms to find.

May health and eaſe her guardian cares attend:
Happy through life, be happier in her end!
Supremely bleſt! who ſees, with virtuous pride,
Her conſort's loſs by filial love ſupplied:
Beholds the patriot deeds and honours, won
By her lov'd Lord, freſh-blooming in her ſon.

---

* A beautiful Urn of white marble (by Mr. Bacon) in the midſt of a laurel grove; the elegance of which ſcene can be exceeded by nothing but by the delicacy of the inſcription, equal to any thing in the Engliſh language.

† Her Ladyſhip's daughter, married to the Hon. E. J. Eliot.

A
SKETCH FROM NATURE.

WRITTEN AT

A SMALL GOTHIC VILLA,

In the moſt beautiful, though leaſt frequented, part of Glouceſterſhire.

AMIDST primæval groves, ſublimely great,
Here Nature fix'd of old her favourite ſeat;
Hence views, with placid mien, the ſubject plain,
The various beauties of her wide domain:
Woods, lawns, neat villages, and farms, ſurveys,
Such ſcenes as Wotton's fertile vale diſplays.
Induſtrious peaſants there contented live
In all the bliſs that health and peace can give;
No demagogues Utopian ſyſtems frame,
Nor furious conteſts rage 'mongſt 'ſquires for game;
But all, on due ſubordination's plan,
In peace enjoy the *ſocial* " rights of man."

The poor, by wealth *employ'd*, and not oppreſs'd,
Are fed, protected, and with plenty bleſs'd:
The rich unenvied, while their plenteous ſtore
With liberal hand 's imparted to the poor.
All taſte, remote from life's fantaſtick ſhow,
The genuine ſweets, which nature's gifts beſtow.

But, if the friendſhip of our worthy hoſt,
Lord of theſe woods and Gothic towers, you boaſt;
Beneath his roof you'll all theſe bleſſings find,
Peace, plenty, ſocial mirth, and virtue join'd.
There ſtill true hoſpitality abides,
And beauty at the feſtive board preſides;
Attentive to each gueſt, her ſmiles imparts,
She feaſts our ſenſes, and ſubdues our hearts.

October 1791.

TO

*MRS. * * * * *,

C**BE-GROVE.

IMPROMPTU.

I BEG, dear Madam, you'll excuſe,
The efforts of my ruſtick muſe;
Not all the arguments you bring,
In *palaces* can make her ſing.
Euterpe is a baſhful maid,
Loves ſolitude and rural ſhade;
'Midſt rocks and woods delights to rove,
And ſuch was once your ſweet C**be-Grove.
But now, alas! the ſcene's too bright,
And puts poetick thoughts to flight,

A footman meets you at the gate,
Conducts you to a room of ſtate;

* Requeſting ſome rhymes on her Villa.

On turtle-ſoup, fowl, fiſh, you dine,
Drink claret, or rich Spaniſh wine.
I praiſe your liberal hoſpitality,
(Not always found amongſt our quality.)
The luxury of ſeven and ſeven,
Exalts an epicure to heaven:
But, give a bard his belly full,
Like vulgar mortals he grows dull.
An hungry poet, in a garret,
Will ſing—and prate like any parrot;
But beef and pudding ſink him down,
And level Pindar with a clown:
He dreams no more of nymph or fawn,
Or Dian ranging o'er the lawn;
His thoughts are grov'ling on the earth,
Which never yet gave genius birth.

In ſhort, ſuch ſplendors all around
My feeble faculties confound:
C**be-Gr*ve's no longer now the ſame,
Combe-*Palace* then muſt be its name;
And you are queen, the 'ſquire a king,
And Warton* muſt your praiſes ſing.

---

* Poet-Laureat at that time.

AN

ETYMOLOGY.*

TO

JAMES P***T A*****S, Esq. F. R. S.

WHEN London ſcarce had ſpread ſo far
(Some centuries paſt) as Temple-bar;
And thence to Weſtminſter, 'tis ſaid,
A dirty lane† the traveller led:
And citizens might find an hare
In Groſvenor or in ‡Soho-ſquare;
An heath there was, towards the weſt,
Not then, with flowers,§ by culture dreſt,
Or villas gay, where ſweetly blows,
The gilliflower, the pink and roſe;
But overrun with native *broom*,
Which now is *Bromton-Grove* become.

* See his Anecdotes, p. 81. † See Pennant's London.

‡ The watch-word at the battle of Sedgmore, *ibid.*

§ Now famous for flowers.

There Andrews dwells in learned eaſe,
And, ſkill'd each man of taſte to pleaſe,
He, patiently at home confin'd,*
Inſtructs and entertains mankind.
Collects each flower, with eye diſcerning;
Conceal'd in labyrinths of learning:†
Or executes the generous plan,
Which ‡Hanway's liberal ſoul began:
Or meditates, in manner new,
His country's annals to review.§
Thus watchful o'er the midnight oil,
The world enjoys his virtuous toil:
Like Epicurus, in his garden,
Fair fame his pleaſing taſk rewarding.
In life's calm ſhade, thus truly great,
Ev'n kings might envy his retreat.

---

* With the gout. † His Anecdotes.

‡ For the relief of the poor chimney-ſweepers.

§ A conciſe Hiſtory of England, on a new plan.

ON

A FEMALE ARTIST*

OF

DISTINCTION.

" She ſate like patience on a monument,
" Smiling at grief."——— SHAKESPEARE.

KIND heaven the good will ne'er with griefs oppreſs,
Without ſome balm to ſoften their diſtreſs;
And, for their " corporal ſufferings," oft on thoſe
A double ſhare of mental powers beſtows.
Depriv'd of ſight thus Milton's lofty mind
Excels in bold deſcription all mankind:
While yet a youth, all nature he explor'd,
And thence his mind with rich materials ſtor'd;
Which, heighten'd by ſtrong fancy's pow'rful ray,
The wonders of his paradiſe diſplay.

* A lady of fortune who reſides in Bath, confined by an incurable lameneſs.

Marcia, though long by dire diſeaſe confin'd,
From nature's beauties, yet has ſtor'd *her* mind,
(Like the great bard) before her ſad retreat,
With all that's *rare*, or *beautiful*, or great.*
Hence in her landſkips, hills, dales, rocks, unite,
With woods or lakes, to captivate the ſight;
Her magic pencil raiſes to our view
The paradiſe which Milton's fancy drew.
Amus'd herſelf, the pleaſure ſhe extends,
With ſcenes Elyſian to amuſe her friends;
Who, 'midſt the raptures which her works impart,
Admire her ſenſe, and goodneſs of her heart.
Nay, trebly bleſt, has rais'd a fund, in ſtore
The ſick to ſolace or to feed the poor.†
For Marcia's ſkill aſſumes a nobler name,
And *charity* and *taſte* in her 's the ſame.

Thus, 'midſt affliction's gloom, ſhe ſits ſerene,
While conſcious virtue gilds the lonely ſcene.
Milton, though blind, could nature's charms improve,
Marcia, though lame, through nature's wilds can rove.
Yet, from *his* verſe but fancied ſcenes ariſe:
Her art brings nature's ſelf before our eyes.

---

* The three ſources of the pleaſures of imagination.

† The ſick and impriſoned have been relieved from that fund.

THE

GENEROUS ŒCONOMIST.

WITH beauty, ſenſe, and fortune bleſt,
And much admir'd, and much careſs'd;
Yet Laura, wonderful to tell,
Has bid th' admiring world farewell:
Frequents no concert, play, or ball,
And, as for routs—ſhe hates them all.
Nor does ſhe, warm in pleaſure's chace,
Purſue her game from place to place:
Now, idly poſting up to town,
Now, reſtleſs hurrying gladly down.
No: Laura grudges the expence—
Yet think her not ſo void of ſenſe,
That, while ſo young, ſhe can at once
Pleaſures of every kind renounce.
Laura, like many a nymph of faſhion,
Still gratifies her ruling paſſion:
Not like ſome pious dames of old,
As by our comick bards we're told;

Who kept lock'd up, amongſt their tea,
A ſip of Nantes* or Ratafia:
Nor does ſhe laviſh her regards
On monkies, lap-dogs, or on cards;
Nor yet preſerve a ſecret part
For ſome fond lover—in her heart.
No: a kind ſpouſe, of her election,
Has long engroſs'd her whole affection.

"What then can this retirement mean?
"'Tis Laura's intereſt to be ſeen."

Be it then rightly underſtood,
Her luxury is—in doing good;
Though Laura 's frugal on herſelf,
Think her not bent on hoarding pelf.
Laura is generous—though ſhe's wiſe,
Frugality her fund ſupplies:
When charities her aid demand,
Laura extends a liberal hand.
With what you diſſipate on dreſs,
She cheers a neighbour in diſtreſs;
With what on *muſick* you employ,
She "makes the widow *ſing* for joy."

* A liquor made in France, uſed medicinally.

Yet, to herſelf and heaven alone,
Her acts of charity are known;
She leaves the world its noiſe and ſhow,
In ſilent ſtreams her bounties flow:
Of heartfelt joys ſhe'll find a ſtore,
When youth and beauty are no more.

Nov, 20, 1792.

VOLTAIRE's VISIT

TO

CONGREVE.*

ERE France, intent on her Utopian plan,
Had ſpurn'd all laws t' aſſert "the rights of man,"
On liberty ſo zealouſly employ'd,
Both liberty and property deſtroy'd;
She long had view'd, with envy—and applauſe,
The matchleſs ſyſtem of our Britiſh laws;
When young *Voltaire*, by freedom's charms inſpir'd,
To freedom's ſeat from deſpotiſm retir'd.

Here heroes he beheld, who bravely fought;
Patriots, who wiſely plann'd or greatly thought;
Philoſophers and bards of glorious name,
Pope who poſſeſs'd, *Young* riſing into fame:
Congreve had long the temple's height attain'd,
Yet ſcorn'd the art by which that height he gain'd.

* See Johnſon's Lives of the Engliſh Poets.

Voltaire, by laudable ambition led
To view the bard whoſe works he oft' had read,
Now introduced, the youth with rapture fir'd,
Expreſs'd how much the *poet* he admir'd!

" Young man! ſays *Congreve*, you're of France I find;
But poliſh'd manners and a liberal mind
Unite us all:—yet you're deceiv'd, I fear,
'Tis as a *gentleman* I ſee you here."

Sir! quoth Voltaire, we've *gentlemen* in France,
Who dreſs, and bow, talk politicks, and—dance;
But you are more—and *therefore* am I come:
And were you not, ſir, I had ſtay'd at home.

ON

MADAME SISLEY,

A

FRENCH LADY OF FORTUNE,

FORCED TO QUIT HER NATIVE COUNTRY, ON THE REVOLUTION, AND TO SING IN PUBLICK FOR A MORE DECENT SUBSISTENCE.

I.

" MUSICK has charms (ſo poets ſay)
  " To ſoothe a ſavage breaſt,"
And beauty's univerſal ſway
  Ev'n tyrants have confeſs'd.

II.

Is it then true, (what we are told)
  That Frenchmen could oppreſs;
That Frenchmen could, unmov'd, behold
  Such beauty in diſtreſs?

III.

Alas! ſuch foul diſhonour ſtains
 That, once, more gallant race:
Deaf to fair Siſley's heavenly ſtrains,
 Blind to her lovely face.

IV.

But Britons to ſuch powers united,
 More juſt, more generous prove:
To rapture by her notes excited,
 And by her charms to love.

21ſt Nov. 1791.

TO

DAVID H*****Y, Esq.

ON

HIS INGENIOUS DISCOVERY

FOR THE

TEMPERING STEEL.

DAVID! who boaſts, with true Vulcanian ſkill,
To make e'en ſteel obedient to thy will;
To every tool its trueſt temper lend,
The ſoft to harden, or the brittle bend:—
See Chloe! when but fancied woe appears,
With infant ſoftneſs melting into tears.
But when her lover for compaſſion ſues,
Unmov'd the ſuppliant ſwain the fair one views:
E'en for her lap-dog tenderly ſhe ſighs,
And pities Pompey—while her lover dies.

Exert then, David, thy Promethean art,
And give conſiſtent feelings to her heart;
Compaſſionate the torments that we feel,
And temper Chloe—as you temper ſteel.

TASTE A-LA-MODE,

1791.

TO

THE HON. MR. N****.

WITH genius, wit, and learning bleſt,
Young N**th the tragick muſe addreſs'd.
He choſe his ſubject; ſketch'd his plan;
And now triumphantly began.

"Ah! cries a friend, (who knew the Town)
"A tragedy will ne'er go down;
"Theſe merry times like nothing ſerious,
"Ev'n Otway now begins to weary us.
"We talk of *feelings*; but you'll find
"They're feelings of a different kind:
"Even Shakeſpeare's ſelf, in this bleſt age,
"Diſguſted, muſt deſert the ſtage."

Well then, if folks don't love to cry,
We now a comick ſcene will try—

Follies abound, and ſure with eaſe
This *merry* town a bard *may* pleaſe.

" Alas! ev'n here, perhaps, my friend,
" You're not ſo ſure to gain your end:
" You'll learn, I fear, ſir, to your coſt,
" Our taſte for *comick humour*'s loſt.
" We want ſome ſweet romantick tale,
" Or *Congreve*'s ſterling wit muſt fail.
If that's the caſe, quoth N****, by chance,
My tale would make a good romance.

" But, ſir, without ſome ſprightly ſong,
" You'll yet ſee every thing go wrong:
" Duets and trios we muſt have,
" For nothing elſe your *play* will ſave.

Quoth N**** (perplex'd with all his wit,
The town's fantaſtick taſte to hit)
'Zounds! here then, take a threefold piece,
Though quite unknown to Rome or Greece:
And, blame not *me*, ye criticks ſage,
But mend the manners of the age:
Were they content with wholſome food,
I'd give them what is freſh and good;
But if with traſh they *will* be cramm'd—
Let them—and all their plays—be *d-mn'd!

* In a theatrical ſenſe.

JUVENILITIES,

EPIGRAMS,

&c.

JUVENILITIES.

DOMESTICK HAPPINESS.

WRITTEN 1750.*

I.

THOUGH chill deſcends the drizzling rain,
And hollow blows the wind:
Of wintry ſtorms I'll not complain,
While thus my Lucy's kind.

II.

When, round my cot, the dreary fields,
And ſhrubs are clad with ſnow,
More joy than ſummer's ſunſhine yields
Her cheering ſmiles beſtow.

* The author was afraid to hazard the ſimplicity of this ballad, forty years ago; but "domeſtick happineſs" is now the *ton*—I mean in novels and romances.

III.

I heed not ruthlefs wars alarms,
That Europe's fons annoy;
While I, fecure of Lucy's charms,
Domeftick peace enjoy.

IV.

For wealth to India's diftant fhore
Let greedy merchants roam;
With Lucy bleft, I afk no more
Than competence at home.

V.

Give epicures their fumptuous fare,
Whilft I, more truly bleft;
The neat, though frugal, viands fhare,
My Lucy's hands have drefs'd.

VI.

The flaunting nymphs, that haunt the town,
I, void of envy, fee;
While Lucy, in her linen gown,
Is all the world to me.

ABSENCE.*

WHILE thus I range theſe ſylvan ſhades,
'Midſt murmuring ſtreams and opening glades,
And liſten to the thrilling notes
Where warbling linnets pour their throats;
Each care, each paſſion lull'd to reſt,
What tranquil pleaſures fill my breaſt!

But ah! what means, as I advance,
This ſigh, that wakes me from my trance?
The linnet now I joyleſs hear,
For ah! my Julia is not there.
How fade the beauties of the grove,
When not enjoy'd with her I love.

In vain the nightingale and thruſh
Their carols chaunt on every buſh;
Her mate the cooing turtle calls,
The ſilver current tinkling falls;
Elyſian ſcenes inſipid prove,
When abſent from the nymph I love.

* Set to muſick by Mr. Rauzzini.

THE

PARTING SOLDIER;*

OR,

THE ELOQUENCE OF TEARS.

I.

WHEN beauty pleads with artleſs ſmiles,
She oft' the ſtouteſt heart beguiles;
But join'd with Daphne's wit and ſenſe,
Who could reſiſt ſuch eloquence?

II.

Nicander could:—he turn'd away:
"'Tis Honour calls, he muſt obey."
And Daphne, deck'd in all her charms,
He thruſt reluctant from his arms.

III.

Again the nymph her rhetorick tries,
With ſuppliant hands and moiſtening eyes;
The ſilent tear ſtole down her cheek,
She ſigh'd, ſhe wept—but could not ſpeak.

* A general officer.

IV.

Her melting tears the hero view'd,
And now his courage was ſubdued:
Honour avaunt! we will not part,
My Daphne's tears o'erpower my heart.

V.

Rous'd from her trance, o'erwhelm'd with ſhame,
And anxious for Nicander's fame,
A crimſon bluſh ſuffus'd her face,
She loos'd him from her fond embrace.

VI.

Ah! go, ſhe cried: Nicander, go!
Nor let *me* prove thy deadlieſt foe:
Nor to my weakneſs ſacrifice
What ſoldiers more than life ſhould prize.

1788.

ON

A VERY YOUNG LADY,

OF

EQUAL WIT AND BEAUTY.

"TOLLE CUPIDINEM IMMITIS UVÆ." HOR.

I.

HOW ſweetly blooms yon opening roſe!
What charms her purple leaves diſcloſe!
Yet, would you raſhly crop the flower,
A thorn exerts its guardian power.

II.

Thus Stella blooms with native charms,
And with fond hopes each boſom warms:
But, though vain fops fear no reſiſtance,
Her wit ſtill keeps them at a diſtance.

III.

Submiſſive then the nymph adore,
Enjoy her ſmiles, and aſk no more—
Her charms by time matur'd, you'll find
Her *wit* will teach her to be kind.

TO

MISS S**M**R.

I.

HER artleſs notes! when Delia ſings,
What raptures they impart!
Or when ſhe ſtrikes the trembling ſtrings,
They vibrate to the heart.

II.

The blended tints her ſkill diſplay,
When ſhe the needle plies—
The linnet flutters on the ſpray,*
The roſe with nature vies.

III.

But words, alas! are all too faint
(Were I to *beauty* blind)
Each virtue and each grace to paint,
Conſpicuous in her *mind.*

* A beautiful piece of needle-work.

IV.

Good ſenſe, with a deſire to pleaſe,
  And condeſcenſion ſweet;
And dignity, with native eaſe,
  In due aſſemblage meet.

V.

In Delia thus, ſo nobly born,
  Theſe qualities abound:
Yet more the fair one to adorn,
  With modeſty they 're crown'd.

VI.

Unconſcious of her charms, the maid
  Thus humble though we view:
More homage than to thrones is paid,
  Fair Delia is thy due.

Seend, June 1789.

EPIGRAMS, &c.

MARTIAL

SPECTAC. LIB. EPIG. II.

TO VESPASIAN.*

WHERE yon ſublime Coloſſus braves the ſkies,
And vaſt machines† with ſelf-mov'd ſtages riſe,
A ſavage tyrant's palace, one proud dome,
Itſelf a city, ſtood alone in Rome.

* The tyrant Nero having demoliſhed almoſt one-third of Rome, to erect his "Golden Palace" as he called it, (conſiſting of porticos near a mile in extent, a coloſſal ſtatue of himſelf 120 feet high; lakes, parks, and woods, ſtocked with wild and tame beaſts of every kind) the Emperors Veſpaſian and Titus deſtroyed it, and built the magnificent amphitheatre, which ſtill remains; put the head of Apollo on the Coloſſus in the place of Nero's,

Where the wide lake its ſtagnant waters ſpread,
An amphitheatre now lifts its head,
See! publick baths erected, where before
Waſte lawns uſurp'd the manſions of the poor:
On the court's utmoſt verge, a grand arcade
Affords at noon its hoſpitable ſhade.
Rome to itſelf by Cæſar now reſtor'd,
Delights a nation—not *one* worthleſs lord.

Nero's, and erected porticos and publick baths for the uſe of the people.——If the unhappy Louis XVI. had followed his own inclination, and, on his acceſſion to the throne, had effected ſome more important popular acts, he might probably have ſaved himſelf and his country from the preſent diſtracted ſituation.

† Some wooden machines for the uſe of the amphitheathre, I believe, to amuſe the populace.

ON THE DEATH OF

JAMES COLLINGS, Esq.

FEB. 1788, AT BATH.

IMITATED FROM MARTIAL, B. i. EP. 40.

Is there a man, like thoſe diſtinguiſh'd few
For friendſhip fam'd whom happier ages knew;
His mind with ſcience ſtor'd, with claſſick taſte,
And true ſimplicity of manners grac'd;
Of ſtricteſt honour and to virtue dear,
Who form'd no wiſh, but all mankind might hear:*
Such was the man, whoſe loſs his friends deplore:
Such Collings was—†but is, alas! no more.‡

* Alluding to the ſecret prayers of the hypocrites. Hor.

† The word *Diſpeream* is too familiar for this occaſion—but may be excuſed in the following imitation.

‡ This character was brought to the author's memory, by the recent death of the worthy Mr. Hoare, to whom it is ſtrictly applicable.

MARTIAL,

BOOK i. EP. 40. IMITATED.

IMPROMPTU

HAVE you not ſeen, to Dover poſting down,
My curious friend, about ten miles from town,
If to the right you haply caſt your eyes,
A ſplendid villa's front majeſtick riſe?
Where, 'midſt the verdant lawn, pavilions gay,
And ſculptur'd urns,* the owner's taſte diſplay?
Where wood and water harmoniz'd unite,
And many a rural object charms the ſight?
Neat cottages and farms the landſkip grace,
But more—the happy peaſant's ruddy face
And healthy, cheerful looks, adorn the ſcene?—
Hang me† if 'tis not D—nſ—n that you mean.

* One, a beautiful antique marble urn, brought from Rome, with its pedeſtal 10 or 12 feet high.

† Diſpeream, ſi non &c.

DECLAMAS BELLE', &c.

MODERNIZED.

YES, you're a *pretty* preacher, ſir, we know it,
Write *pretty* **novels*, are a *pretty* poet;
A *pretty* critick, and tell *fortunes*† too;
Then, who writes farce or epigrams like you?
At every ball how *prettily* you nick it:
You fiddle, ſing, play *prettily* at cricket.
Yet, after all, in nothing you excel,
Do all things *prettily*, but nothing *well.*
What ſhall I call you?—Say the beſt I can,
You are, my friend, a ‡*very buſy* man.

---

* Bellas hiſtorias. † Bellus es aſtrologus.

‡ Magnus es Ardelio. Αυλώτατος.

AN

EXPENSIVE JILT.

B. XI. EP. 50.

" HÆC NÔSSE SALUS EST ADOLESCENTULIS." TER.

THERE's not an hour, my Phillis, in the day,
But you contrive to make my fondneſs pay.
Your maid, an artful ſlut, now cries, " Alas!
" What ſhall I do?—I've broke my lady's glaſs.
Then Phillis comes herſelf, in tears, poor thing!
And tells me ſhe has loſt her favourite ring,
Or dropt, perchance, a diamond from her locket—
Then, a new piece of ſilk muſt *pick my pocket.
Behold her next, her eſſence-box produce,
Which wants ſome rich perfume or eau-de-luce.
Now an old hag, pretending to divine
And ſolve her dreams, muſt have ſome old tent wine: †
I then for fiſh the market muſt explore,
Some demirep will dine with us at four.

* Furtiva lucri.

† " *Nigra*," to appeaſe the infernal deities.

But, prithee! Phillis, pay ſome ſmall regard
To juſtice—and my generous love reward:
Since I *refuſe* you nothing, how can you
Thus pick my pocket—and *refuſe** me too?

TO

MISS S**** H*******.

CECILIA ſings:—how ſtrong, how clear,
Her thrilling accents ſtrike the ear!
But, by degrees, the ſoften'd lay
In melting ſweetneſs dies away:
And, while we liſten to the fair,
The notes ſeem half-diſſolv'd in air.
Yet ſuch the raptures they impart,
With lightning's force they pierce the heart.

* "*Negas.*" Verbum amatorium.

MARTIAL,

PAUPER CINNA VULT VIDERI—ET EST PAUPER,

IMITATED.

WITH old ſlouch'd hat and undreſs'd hair,
Cinna affects a ruſtick air;
And, while due forms he thus neglects,
He is the *ruſtick* he affects.

ANOTHER.

Callidus impoſuit nuper mihi caupo Ravennæ,
Cum peterem mixtum, vendidit ille merum.

IMITATED: A REAL FACT.

Indeed, my good friend, I have cauſe to complain,
When I call'd for ſome cyder, you gave me Champagne.

ON

TEMPERANCE.

Πλέον ἥμισυ παντός.* HES.

YOU dine with lords, and with insulting air,
Repeat, in savoury terms, your bill of fare:
I, happy to escape a sumptuous treat,
Enjoy the venison—which I did *not* eat.

ON THE

FRENCH REVOLUTION.

THEY who, impatient of the yoke,
Have driv'n one tyrant from the throne;
Now, to more base submission broke,
Beneath ten thousand tyrants groan.

* "A pint of wine is better than a bottle."

EQUALITY;

OR,

THE DYING LOVER.

YOUNG Corydon, a forward blade,
The offspring of a 'ſquire,
Addreſs'd a lovely, blooming maid,
Whoſe father was—a dyer.

" A Dyer's daughter! cries his dad,
" What! marry her! O fye!"
" Why not, ſir, ſays the honeſt lad,
" You know we all *muſt die.*

AN

USEFUL APOTHEGM

FOR

A FOND MOTHER.

WHETHER charg'd or uncharg'd, I charge you, my ſon,
Never wantonly face the mouth of a gun;
And, tam'd or untam'd, pray likewiſe beware,
Come not nigh to the heels of a horſe or a mare.

OR THUS:

Approach not, I charge you, if danger you'd ſhun,
The heels of a horſe, or the mouth of a gun.

TO A LADY,

WHO MISTOOK THE WORD

APOTHEGM FOR APOZEM.

An *Apozem*, madam, would make your child ſick:
My *Apothegm*—ſave him from many a kick.

THE

CHOICE OF A HUSBAND.

THE SENTIMENTS

OF

A YOUNG LADY.

DON'T marry an *old* man, my father advifes,
To marry a *young* man, mamma thinks unwife is:
An old man is jealous, will be peevifh and teaze you,
A young man is fickle, and will not *long* pleafe you.
That my choice of a hufband may not be thought wrong then,
I'll have nothing to do with old men or young men.
A middle-aged man comes neareft the truth,
With the wifdom of *age* and the ardour of *youth*.
With fuch a one only I ever will marry,
And my hope of true blifs can hardly mifcarry.

IN THE STYLE OF

MASTER THOMAS STERNHOLD,

TOUCHING CRITICKS.

I.

BLEST is the man, who, free from ſtrife,
Can read and write at home!
Enjoy an unambitious life,
Nor vainly wiſh to roam

II.

Where ſinners ply the grey gooſe-quill,
In Critical Reviews;
And verſe or proſe, with dangerous ſkill,
Unfeelingly abuſe.

III.

Ungodly men! on miſchief bent!
Who "ſit in ſcorner's chair,"
And, not to keep eternal Lent,
On harmleſs authors fare.

IV.

But he who by his parlour fire
Right peaceably doth ſit,
Nor ever proudly doth aſpire
To tread the paths of wit;

V.

To criticks deaf as Scilly's rocks,
" Their doings will deride,
" And make them all as mocking-ſtocks,
" Throughout the world ſo wide."

BY

ATTERBURY,

WHEN A

WESTMINSTER SCHOLAR.

On the figure of JUDAS in the Altar-Piece, ſaid to be taken from a well-known character.

FALLERIS hâc te qui pingi ſub imagine, credis,
Non ſimilis Judas eſt tibi—pænituit.*

TRANSLATED.

Think not by Judas *thou* art repreſented,
Though Judas was a thief—yet *he* repented.

* I cannot recollect a more ſevere ſtroke of ſatire, conveyed in ſo few words.

IN OBITUM

DOM. ELIZ. SHERIDAN,

FORMA, VOCE, ATQUE INGENIO,

INTER ORNATAS ORNATISSIMÆ,

AB IMO AMORES ITA SUSPIRAT

AMICUS.

EHEU! EHEU! LUGEANT MORTALES!

EJA VERO GAUDEANT CŒLESTES!

DULCES AD AMPLEXUS,

SOCIANS JAM CITHARÆ MELOS,

REDIT PERGRATA,

EN! ITERUM SOROR;

SUAVIUSQUE NIL MANET *HOSANNIS*.

ON THE

DEATH OF

MRS. SHERIDAN,

FROM

THE LATIN OF DR. H———N.

SURE, every beauty, every grace,
  Which other females ſhare,
Adorn'd thy mind, thy voice, thy face,
  Thou faireſt of the fair!—
Amidſt the general diſtreſs,
Oh! let a friend his grief expreſs!

Yet whilſt, alas! each mortal mourns,
  Rejoice! ye heavenly Choir!
To your embraces ſhe returns;
  And, with her ſocial lyre,
ELIZA* now reſumes her ſeat,
And makes your harmony compleat.

---

* Original "SOROR."

TO

AN IRISH GENTLEMAN.†

A CARD,

DECLINING AN INVITATION

TO

A CONVERSAZIONI.

SAINT Patrick's dean, though deaf, was *Swift*,
I'm deaf, alas! but ſlow:
True wit and humour were his gift,
But not *my* gift, *you* know.

As well might one that could not eat
Attend your jovial cheer,
As I diſturb your higher treat
Of wit, I cannot hear.

† The late worthy Dr. Domville.

WRITTEN AFTER A

CONVIVIAL ENTERTAINMENT.

SATUR EST CUM DICIT HORATIUS EVÆ.

JUV.

THE Sheriff, to convene a county meeting,
To *gentlemen* and *clergy* ſendeth greeting:
Hinting in each a different ſtyle of breeding,
Of birth, of rank—and elegance of feeding.

But thoſe that dine with *K—— will ſee, delighted;
In him theſe various qualities united;
And find, as we this cheerful day have done,
The *Gentleman* and *Clergyman* in one.

* A reverend and worthy baronet.

HEROICK LOVE:

A DIALOGUE BETWEEN

DON QUIXOTE AND SANCHO PANCHA,

IN THE BROWN MOUNTAIN,

(When the ſquire returned from his embaſſy to Lady Dulcinea.)

WELL, Sancho, I confeſs indeed,
Like a good ſquire thou'ſt made good ſpeed:*
Come! ſooth my anxious boſom's void,
And tell me how my love's employ'd.
Is ſhe intent on ſtringing pearls
To decorate her auburn curls,
Or making up her Bruſſels lace
To ſhade the beauties of her face?
Was ſhe amidſt the myrtle grove
Weaving the ſtory of our love;
Or, on a moſſy bank reclin'd,
Soothing with books her penſive mind;

* The joke was, inſtead of going three days journey to Toboſo the ſquire returned with the curate and barber.

The roſe and violet round her blooming,
With fragrant ſcents the air perfuming?

No, no: I ſaw no pearls or roſes,
Or ſuch fine things as you *ſuppoſes*:
I found your ſweetheart winnowing wheat,
All cover'd o'er with duſt and ſweat;
And, when I told her you were dying
For love of her, inſtead of crying,
The ſaucy ſlut began to titter:
But when I gave her your kind letter,
She laid it down upon the ſack,
And ſaid, I'd better take it back:
" For faith and troth!" the poor wench ſaid,
" I never learn'd to write or read;
" But if he longs to kiſs my toe ſo,
" Let 'en come and do it at Toboſo."

So, pleaſe your worſhip, my good maſter,
For fear of ſome more dire diſaſter;
Let us no longer through thoſe highlands,
In queſt of governments or iſlands,
Or killing giants, idly roam,
But mount our ſteeds—and travel home.

A

CHARACTER, 

IN THE MANNER OF *CHAUCER.*

A Wight there was, ſcarce known I ween to fame,
Who day by day to Bathe's fam'd city came:
Meagre, and very rueful were his looks,
He ſeem'd as he had fed on naught but books.
His old great coat, " which he could ne'er forſake,
" Hung half before and half behind his back."
Full threeſcore ſprings had bloſſom'd o'er his head,
Yet nimble as a roebuck was his tread:
For, * in his youth he ne'er did heat his blood
With liquors hot, or high and luſcious food.
Therefore his age like froſty winter paſt,
Hoary, but hale; and healthy to the laſt.
" What! walk to Bath, ſir?" cries ſome gouty man;
" No, ſir, quoth he, I did not *walk*—I *ran.*"

---

* Shakeſpeare.

He ſtroll'd about, and travers'd many a ſtreet:
Eftſoons ſome friend or dainty nymph wou'd greet:
With ſcornful looks, by empty fops ſurvey'd
By ſcornful looks or ſneers, he undiſmay'd
On matters deep or mus'd or ſeem'd to muſe,
Then made an halt, then read or heard the news;
Bought ſome old book or print perchance, and then,
Small buſineſs done, he travell'd home again.

Such is the life of man, with buſy face,
On trifles bent, he ſtrolls from place to place;
With various ſcenes of happineſs amus'd,
By turns applauded—and by turns abus'd.
To ſorrow's ſchool ſent weeping from the womb,
Spends his ſhort ſpan—then haſtens to the tomb:
Life's but a morning's lounge, unleſs confin'd
To duty's path, and uſeful to mankind.

ON THE

APPROACH OF WINTER.

ALAS! with what unwearied ſpeed
  Revolves the circling year!
Seaſons to ſeaſons ſtill ſucceed—
  Appear and diſappear.

The Spring, on balmy zephyrs borne,
  With roſes blooming round;
The Summer deck'd with ears of corn,
  With fruits the Autumn crown'd;

Again are fled—and o'er the dawn
  Now murky fogs ariſe:
The ſun but faintly gilds the lawn,
  Then haſtens down the ſkies.

The groves their leafy honours ſhed,
  No more their warblers ſing:
Each inſect ſeeks his wintry bed,
  To wait returning ſpring.

The plaintive Swallow now prepares
To ſeek ſome milder ſhore;
A gloomy face all nature wears,
And pleaſure is no more.

Thus fly the cheerful days of man,
Dull cares his thoughts engage:
Each hour contracts his little ſpan,
And hurries on Old Age.

Wrinkles his brow, grey hairs his head,
Sharp pains his limbs invade:
His ſpirits flag, his mirth is fled,
And all his proſpects fade.

From crowds, on airy projects bent,
Let me in time retire;
And, with domeſtick ſcenes content,
Enjoy my winter's fire.

No more from flower to flower I'll range,
But wait in calm repoſe;
A torpid inſect, till my change
Some happier ſtate diſcloſe.

While thus the ſeaſons reſtleſs roll,
And naught is conſtant here,
To endleſs bliſs Hope wafts the ſoul
Beyond the ſtarry ſphere.

MARTIAL

LIB. i. EP. 10.

AD LIBRUM.

Argiletanas mavis habitare tabernas;
Cum tibi, parve liber, scrinia nostra vacent, &c.

IMITATED.

TO HIS BOOK.

SAFE in my desk, you wish, it seems, to go
To fam'd Pall-Mall—or Pater-noster-Row,
And mount a shelf beneath the splendid works,
Which eternize our Sidneys, Lockes, and—Burkes.
Alas! you know not the fastidious looks,
With which bold Britons* now peruse new books.
Ah! never sure were criticks more severe:
Even school-boys crisp the nose† and learn to sneer.

* Martia turba. † Nasum rhinocerotis.

www.ingramcontent.com/pod-product-compliance
Lightning Source LLC
Chambersburg PA
CBHW030328270326
41926CB00010B/1539
9783744689397